CYNTHIA BAKER

Still Stuck

It's not a mystery. It's your mindset. Revealing the mystery and the missing steps to lasting change.

PLATYPUS
PUBLISHING

First edition

Editing by Curt Baker
Editing by Brooke Holt
Proofreading by Caleb Culver
Advisor: Emily Goodin
Advisor: Matt Culver
Cover art by Kerri @ 99 Designs

This book was professionally typeset on Reedsy.
Find out more at reedsy.com

This book was written for you,
with you in mind, because your life matters to God.

I am so thankful to the Lord for opening my eyes
to hope and a different path.

Curt, you are my best encourager, cheerleader and fan.

Mom and Dad for your love and support
throughout each phase in my life.

James for journeying alongside me through the formative years.

Matt, my wonder twin, thank you for the countless hours
spent with me on my journey.
Without that season, I would still be stuck.

Contents

III   Part 3

Acknowledgement

I want to give a special acknowledgment and thanks to the works of Dr. Caroline Leaf. Her work in the book *Switch on Your Brain*, inspired me to press on toward helping people change. The fingerprint of her principles are here in this book. She connected the scriptures and neuroscience in a way I had never seen.

Thank you Dr. Leaf.

I

Part 1

What I wish I knew long before now.

*If I could have told my 12 year old self these things,
I would have. But now it's a part of my story, and I'm
truly thankful.*

*Yours too. Your life up to now is your story.
And you get to change some things. If you want to.*

1

Introduction

I distinctly remember hoping that moving from Texas to San Francisco would magically change me. I was hoping to leave a few things behind, namely some extra weight, my sense of style (or lack thereof), and a boyfriend. To sum it up, exchanging the old me for a new one.

Nearly 30 years later, yes, it's laughable!

There were some changes I wanted to make and, in my mind, moving from Texas to California was how it would happen. In 1994, for the first time, I bumped into an annoying truth that eventually became one of my favorite sayings.

"Wherever you go, there you are!"

Let me translate for you: "You can't get away from yourself!"

Nope. I couldn't. And you can't either.

It's what I would call a cousin to the coaching saying, "The way you do anything is the way you do everything." Meaning, the way you show up in life in one area transfers to most other areas—from your relationships to your work, hobbies, and almost every endeavor you undertake. So, yes, your business, the people in your life, and the clerk checking you out at the store all get the same you.

Let's use me as a guinea pig to explore this idea. I can be very detail-oriented when I want or need to be, but sometimes I can be lazy when it comes to details I don't care about.

I don't read instructions. I never read the manual; I'd rather figure things out on my own or not use one at all. I call the guy at the car place to figure out how to work the sunroof on my new car. I tinker with the remote until either it works, or I give up and turn it off. I never read the fine print on anything, so the number of times I have signed up for some auto-renew subscription is too big to count. The way I show up is I sign up, read the bolded print, and expect someone to walk me through the big things. I am the exception to the rule on everything in fine print. I hate guided tours, some details (especially boring ones), instructions, excess paper, anything that requires a magnifying glass to read, and doing research—including big purchases like houses and cars. I use most things up to about 45% of their capacity because I never do research.

You are right to be annoyed if you are thinking about how that puts a burden on those around me because I do some things halfway! Reading half of a text because I decide what it's saying before I finish, never reading what I am signing because I assume it only says things I agree with, and counting on others to fill in for the way I avoid details I consider boring are all ways I might not follow through with tasks. And sadly, it's even how I showed up in my work.

For example, I was a professional counselor, and yet, early in my career, I wasn't interested in personality tests, including the in-vogue Myers Briggs. It felt like details and research, and I hated it, even though it was super helpful in understanding the people I was working with.

But when the Enneagram regained popularity, for reasons I don't understand, I fell in love with it. I'm a 7 on the Enneagram scale. What's a 7, you might be asking? Oh, let me share! Desperate to avoid being trapped in emotional pain. Check. Avoiding boredom. Check. Maybe that's a clue as to why I hate manuals and research and treat them like the plague. Prone to addiction. 1,000%—before I went back to school for a degree in Biblical counseling.

I didn't know it at the time, but I was either going to be an addict or an emotionally healthy person. Not much in between. Mainly, I had a quest for understanding why I did what I did and how to deal with it. I had proven that without understanding myself and a different way of operating, too often I found myself in front of the fridge trying to decide what would make me feel better in the moment.

I share these things for two reasons. First, to illustrate that how *you* show up in life is largely a way of doing things. That matters because if there is an area you want to grow in or if you feel stuck, this might be part of a larger mindset or way of operating. One of the keys to making progress in areas you are stuck in is discovering the mindset itself. This one truth has changed my life, and I believe it can change yours, too.

The second reason I share is to tell you that I am 100% a friend traveling alongside you, not a girl who has it together. I don't have it all figured out, but I have learned some things on my own journey that have radically changed my trajectory, and those truths might help you too! One of my favorite ways to spend time is helping people who want to grow. You don't have to move toward more freedom, but you can. And I would venture to guess your life will be more satisfying if you do.

In this book, I will address three things. First, if you are stuck, you will look at removing the mystery behind why. My goal is to convince you that you don't have to stay where you are.

Secondly, in Part Two, you will find four principles of how to get unstuck as well as a few exercises from my coaching curriculum to help you get started.

And lastly, in Part Three, we are going to break this process down into steps to make it simple. That doesn't mean without effort, but it's not hard to move forward if you decide it's worth it to do the work.

But let's start by removing the mystery.

If you are stuck, it's not a mystery. It's your mindset. But it's not that big and it's not that scary.

Although I've used many of my own personal examples throughout the book, hearing from people I have worked with over the
years will be so much more powerful as you see the changes that
happen when you carve out time to work on your mindset!

My hope is that these examples interspersed throughout the
book will help you see how this process has helped many get
from the mindset they had and the results they were unhappy
with to the mindset they wanted and the results of being where
they want to be.

2

Jim's Story

J im struggled with something that many people I coach want more of as well: confidence. Although working on confidence is an intangible goal, it is super important because it affects so much of our everyday life. It affects how we act, talk, and feel about ourselves and then the choices we make, which are usually on a subconscious level. This affects how we come across to people, which ultimately invites people to respond to us in specific ways. There are many roots to this lack of confidence, but we know many times it is rooted in messages and beliefs, some of which true and some of which are just voices from the past. By doing mindset work, you can change how you believe and feel about yourself to be in line with what is true and therefore act or make choices in keeping with those beliefs, which over time produces different results.

Jim first started coaching during the end of a season of work where he was wondering if he was the guy he wanted to be, specifically, the manager type. He was doubting he had the skills and DNA for this role. During our coaching engagement, he was laid off from his current employer and I encouraged him that it was actually the BEST time to do coaching.

(Sidenote: there are many times during the coaching process when people can feel like they need to take a step back and pause their coaching work. This is actually when they need to lean into the discomfort or challenging time. Coaching during hard seasons is an excellent time to evaluate how you are thinking and believing about situations.)

As we processed some of the messages from his childhood, he realized that his doubt came from a deep-seeded wound and belief that had been a part of how he saw himself. Not smart or not smart enough, not the manager type, not the guy, not who he wanted to be. As we moved through a step-by-step process, basically an in-depth version of what has been laid out here for you, he gained clarity on who he actually was, where the beliefs started, and the messages he was believing. As he compared them to the reality of who he had become through his hard work over the years, his confidence changed. It changed when he began to explore and challenge the way he saw himself and compared it to reality. His beliefs changed. Once his beliefs changed, so did the way he showed up with people.

Ultimately, Jim's confidence matched his experience, and he began to see all that he had to offer and ultimately his circumstances changed when he was offered the job he wanted with the company he wanted. In his words:

Coaching through the Link Program uncovered blind spots that were holding me back. I'd originally joined the process as a way of improving areas of my life that I thought held me back I soon discovered there were blind spots I couldn't see that were the real reason I wasn't seeing the positive results in my life that I wanted to see.

This has helped me define my goals better. I know what I'm working on and working towards. Having that clearer path, because of the Link Program, has given me much more confidence and clarity.

3

Why All the Mystery?

T wenty-three years ago, I was just beginning to uncover that I had an eating disorder. When I decided to go back to school and pursue a master's degree, trying to understand myself was at the heart of that educational pursuit. What I can't believe I missed altogether was that my All-or-Nothing Mindset was driving my daily life.

I want to insert a caveat here.

As a professional counselor and now a business coach, I have worked with hundreds of people over the last 20 years who needed healing. And though I wouldn't say that changing your mindset necessarily heals your wounds, what I am saying is that your mindset certainly could have evolved from your wounds, and both healing and working on your mindset are important work.

Over the last 10 years of coaching, I have bumped into people who could not make progress on their goals because they needed healing. I tell you this because you may be reading these words and need healing from childhood wounds, adulthood wounds, things that happened to you, or even choices you made. It takes time to heal those wounds, and if you don't know how to do that, sit with another trusted person or a counselor and let them guide you. I love counselors. I believe in the work they do. They are helping change the landscape of people's lives for the better.

Okay, back to what was shocking to me. Despite years of effort to overcome my own eating disorder, a deeply rooted thought pattern persisted, and it actually invaded every aspect of my life. Remember how we started? A way of showing up in life that crosses over from one area to many other areas. Mine included eating and body image, but it extended to studying, work, growing a business, dating, and relationships—and the list goes on.

Just 10 years ago, I would have simultaneously loved and hated this book. Loved it because someone finally removed the mystery of why I was stuck and hated it because it took away my excuses for staying there. I don't know about you, but I rarely think about how I think and certainly don't realize my thought patterns dictate every single thing I do. Discovering the mindset that has you stuck changes everything because then you can pull it apart, rebuild it, and maybe find a whole new way of living your life.

You may be thinking, "I'm not stuck," or you might feel too busy to pause, let alone stop to work on this. Certainly, you may not be where I was, but I would argue that you probably have an area of your life where you want more. My encouragement to you is that it's worth it. It's worth doing the work to find more in your life. Deeper relationships, more emotional freedom, greater joy, and more peace—basically, a more fulfilling life.

The Secret Life of Walter Mitty is one of my favorite movies of all time. I so highly recommend it that I'll go out on a limb to proclaim it has more life lessons than any other movie I've ever seen—says the girl who didn't read any of the classics. Anyway, Ben Stiller plays a romantic that lives in his own little world because he's too afraid to live in the reality of his own life. Hmmm. Sound familiar? See also any unhealthy obsession we have that hinders our relationships. I digress. He works for a magazine called *Life* and their motto is, "To see the world, things dangerous to come to, to see behind walls, draw closer, to find each other, and to feel. That is the purpose of life."[1]

I share this to tell you that one of my secret life desires is to inspire people to look at their lives. If you are stuck, I want you to both care and want to do something about it. I want to compel you to examine your life, decide what it means for you to live a meaningful life, and then remove the barriers so you can go and do it.

Socrates' saying that an unexamined life isn't worth living resonates deeply in my bones. It is my deepest prayer that this book will compel you to think about *your* life. I hope you will choose to pursue more. To see your everyday as the adventure God has for you and the passions in your heart as what He placed there to live out.

Then, my hope is to help you see why you might be stuck if you're not living them out. The truth is it isn't some big mystery; it's all about your mindset. What a mindset is and how it functions is our next topic.

4

Off to See the Wizard

I never really liked *The Wizard of Oz*. I watched it, but mainly because I felt like I had to. As I was thinking about the best metaphor to describe what I want to communicate, I kept coming back to a vivid picture from the movie: this little band of friends on a journey to see the Wizard. He was a big loud voice in the sky, albeit not an encouraging one, that kept telling them who they were. When they finally arrived and pulled the curtain back, what they saw was shocking. A small man projecting a booming voice through a megaphone-type instrument.

THAT, my friends, is how a mindset functions!

The amplified voice of the Wizard was louder than reality. In fact, it scared everyone (except Toto) into thinking he was bigger than he was and that he had the final word. In the areas of your life you want to change, your mindset is just like the small guy behind the curtain. It is the influential voice in your head, telling you who you are and how to live your life.

You have a mindset around almost everything you do.

Let's use brushing your teeth as an example. Why do you brush or floss? What is your belief? More than likely, it comes from your parents. Even if you are not the child of a dentist, you likely brush and floss daily because you BELIEVE brushing and flossing are crucial to the health of your mouth. It keeps plaque from forming, which makes for healthy gums and gives longevity to your teeth.

Your **beliefs** lead to **feelings.** Of guilt possibly—you probably can't get in bed without your mouth feeling dirty or you think of the plaque hardening overnight. This leads to an **action**: brushing and flossing even if you are tired. This then leads to certain **results**: having a healthy gumline and mouth (unless you are an over-flosser like me, and then you may have receding gums). But that's another issue.

Your mindset has become a way of showing up and living your life. I am defining "mindset" as a collection of categories or parts starting with your thoughts that turn into beliefs followed by feelings and actions, which in turn produce certain results, or the fruit of our actions. It's made up of lots of parts, but it culminates into a way of doing life.

The challenge with a mindset is seeing it.

Seeing the mindsets that drive you takes work because they boot up like a computer when you wake up. We all have mindsets that have helped us succeed and mindsets that have led us to failure. For the purposes of this book, we are focusing on the areas that you are stuck in or want to see growth.

Before this is over, we are going to pull back the curtain and give you the opportunity to dismantle *your* own wizard's voice in the area you want to make progress. Just like the Wizard was hidden behind a curtain, your mindsets are truly hidden, under the radar, and buried in the recesses of your brain.

They often go unnoticed and unchallenged, running your life without a fight and yet determining the way you see your life and the world.

Why your mindset is hidden is our next topic. And we'll get to how to dismantle and rebuild it in Part Two.

5

My Brain Is More Genius Than I Am

I t's amazing that I have a brain and yet I don't understand it. Neuroscience is baffling to my brain. Dr. Caroline Leaf is an expert in the field, and I've decided she's brilliant. In her book *Switch on Your Brain*, she talks about ideas like quantum physics. Although I couldn't mentally grasp all she laid out, reading this was life-changing because it affirmed what I had been seeing and experiencing related to change. Her research influenced many of the principles we will tackle in Part Two. So, lest you fall asleep during our biology portion of the book, let me illustrate simply why it is SUPER important we understand a few things about the brain.

I'll use working out as our example. We all know we can't go to the gym, work out once, and have the physique we saw in the magazine earlier in the day. Why? Because there is a law at work in the universe and it is there whether we acknowledge it or not. We have to do behaviors over time to reap the results we want. You all know this saying: "You reap what you sow." It's called the law of sowing and reaping, and it's there whether we believe it to be true or not. We don't and can't get results overnight.

You are probably asking, "What is the point you are trying to make here?"

There are principles related to how our brains work, laws at work just like sowing and reaping, that directly affect your ability to change! What I want you to hear is this. If you miss this, you might go through life thinking you are forever stuck in the identity and role you have always played, when you actually are not! **You don't have to stay in the place you are unless the place you are is worth putting down your roots. You can change.**

So, we are going to focus on two concepts that highlight our brain and its phenomenal ability to change.

On to concept number one. Whether you live in the boonies or in the middle of a big city, the overload of stimuli you encounter every day is a fact. The people, places, and things you come across—unless, of course, you are a hermit—are infinite. In order to keep our heads from exploding or moving on a swivel, our brains filter out what is important to us by suppressing distracting stimuli that are perceived to be unimportant.[2]

Our brain's goal is to help us survive. Where the sorting hat in *Harry Potter* sorted people, our brains sort data. Is this person, place, or thing important to my survival? When I see a book laying on a table at Starbucks entitled *Engineering for Dummies*, my brain doesn't notice or give it a second thought. Well, maybe my brain says, "I'm so glad I don't need to read that because it sounds like a yawner." But if I walk by a table that has a book entitled *Mindset, Blah Blah Blah* I do a double take. I might even stop and ask its owner if it's good or what it's about because it could be important to my thriving.

Our brains weed out the important from the unimportant to get us through a day. They inform us when we walk out in front of an oncoming car, and they are geniuses at taking out the unnecessary pieces on our game board of life. See also: me and engineering.

Now onto concept two. In the same vein, there are a million things we could be doing so our brains work to make life as automatic as possible. It is widely known that our brains have the ability to go on autopilot; in other words, our brains create habits. I am not sure how it happens, but it has something to do with the basal ganglia. Summarized in the article *Your Brain's Autopilot Function*, deep down our brains are working to create habits that remove our thinking and motivation. "The basal ganglia, a group of structures found deep within your brain, is activated when you perform habits. Because habits run on autopilot, they don't interact much with motivation. That's why changing a habit can be so challenging, even if you feel motivated."[3]

Our habits develop what we call neural pathways in the brain. The article "The Neuroscience of Behavior Change" describes the relationship between habits and neural pathways. Don't tune out yet! It's crucial that you get the big picture here. "Neural pathways, comprised of neurons connected by dendrites, are created in the brain based on our habits and behaviors. The number of dendrites increases with the frequency a behavior is performed. I picture these neural pathways as deep grooves or roads in our brain."[4]

Remember the brushing-your-teeth example? How many of you have a strategy around deciding to brush? Nope. Not me. I have two triggers that remind me I need to do this: heading to bed at night or getting up in the morning. No thought, no resistance, no energy spent.

I'd like to thank my coaching trainer, Dr. Jane Gardner, for the perfect metaphor to illustrate the formation of neural pathways.[5] Let's explore the idea of sledding for a moment.

You wake up one morning to find new snow on the ground. Living in Texas, you rarely see snow and are giddy about wearing snow gear. In a hurry not to miss the occasion, you make a cup of coffee, throw on those fun-but-slightly-snug clothes, and grab a sled from the garage. You are out to enjoy the morning. After all that, you finally find a little untouched hill. Hauling yourself and your sled up to the top, you set the sled down and hop on for the first ride of the day. Down the hill you go. Arriving at the bottom, you look up to see the trail you created. Oh, that was fun! So, you head back up to do it again.

There was a slight trail on the first go, and over the course of the morning, it turned into a packed and bumpy rut by lunchtime. Now if you set your sled down even close to the old rut, down the hill you go, slipping right back into it. And BAM! You screech to a halt in the same place.

So it is with your brain. What do I mean by that? The way I

understand it is, this is how your neural pathways are formed. When we participate in something—including our thoughts, beliefs, and feelings—and act on it, the neural pathways are in the process of forming. Psychologist Deann Ware, Ph.D., explains it this way: "When brain cells communicate frequently, the connection between them strengthens and 'the messages that travel the same pathway in the brain over and over begin to transmit faster and faster.' With enough repetition, these behaviors become automatic. Reading, driving, and riding a bike are examples of complicated behaviors that we do automatically because neural pathways have formed."[6] This is how things become automatic or habitual, again, so your brain can make things mindless.

The first time you do anything, there is a slight trail but as you repeat the thought, feeling, and action, it becomes a well-worn pathway. That's why Gretchen Rubin warns us to pay careful attention to how we do something the first time we do it in her book *Better Than Before*. After the first time, it becomes a pathway in our brain and eventually, down the road, a habit.[7]

I've coached people over the years who had to work on changing their ways of operating because they weren't aware of the consequences to their brains when they made those initial small choices. I remember right after reading Rubin's book and hearing her speak, I started working in Houston once a month. Unfortunately, I loathe boredom, plus I am a stopper and a snacker. What that means is a repeated road trip that's more than 90 miles can be a quick way to pack on a few pounds. As I got in my car for the first time to head down the interstate from Dallas, I remembered the principle that doing something the first time creates a pathway.

I remember thinking, "Okay it's my first time to make this drive, and I need to create a way to get to Houston that doesn't end in tight pants and more time in the gym." I went into the convenience store and grabbed a bag of Skinny Pop! Popcorn, or maybe it was sunflower seeds, and a drink and off I went. Guess what? It worked! That became my new habit. But the opposite is absolutely true too. Let me count the ways I created a bad habit because I wasn't aware of the consequences to my brain.

Back to brushing your teeth. Hopefully, brushing your teeth is an ingrained habit. If it is, it's likely something you do that doesn't require a lot of thought or willpower; you just do it because of the event or action preceding or following, like waking up (event preceding) or going to bed (event following). How? Because over the years, your brain dumbed it down as you created neural pathways to make tooth brushing automatic, minimizing the energy spent on it.

Tactic two of making things automatic is accomplished through developing neural pathways and the ability to form new ones. This is called neuroplasticity. Pay attention here. This is *muy importante* because THIS is your hope for change!

Scientists have actually observed on their own how God created our brains to work. What they found is that our brains are malleable and regenerate themselves by making new synapses. Meaning, our brains make new connections every day, close to 1,000 per day even as we age.[8] Which means we can rewire our brains to make new habits and actions automatic.

Here is the main point of all of this: your brain can change the results and habits you have now! We'll talk more about Dr. Leaf's thoughts later, but she says our brain doesn't distinguish between good and bad habits or pathways.[9] What?! As you may have figured out already, these principles work both for and against us.

Why does that matter? If you have a habit you need to quit because it has become automatic and it gives you the fruit or results that you don't like, you can change it! And you can even put a new one in its place that can become just as automatic over time.

Let's summarize two of the tactics your brain uses to make it in this world. Your brain has too many things to process to be thinking about brushing your teeth every day, so it weeds out the unimportant. In addition to that, it uses its ability to create new pathways to make as many things as automatic as possible. Okay, now what does this chapter have to do with mindsets?

In the area of your life in which you want to grow or change, your beliefs, thoughts, and actions have become automatic and then this has led to fruit **you don't want in your life**. THIS is the reason this chapter is important! The collection of parts, a.k.a. your mindset, has become automatic.

Our next point of exploration is how these mindsets are formed.

6

How Mindsets Form

Our mindsets are formed in many ways, and we are going to talk about a few of them.

If you have kids, you know that training their brains can be a daily whipping—for both you and them. It takes time and persistence to create habits for your kids. Why? Those neural pathways we discussed in Chapter 3 don't create deep ruts over overnight. We will come back to research later that says it takes 10,000 repetitions to master something. However, once the neural pathway has developed into a rut, it's there and the lion's share of your work is done.

Which is great if the habit you created is giving you the results you want.

Let's take the teeth-brushing example to illustrate a point I want to make even further.

Why do you brush your teeth?

I'm pausing to give you a minute. Seriously. Think about why and how?

Your tooth-brushing habits are likely established now because early in your life, you took on someone else's influence whether brushing your teeth was important or not. You might think it is done a certain way or it's prompted by certain things, like getting up or going to bed. Your parents may have told you one of several things about brushing your teeth: it's part of good hygiene, good breath or keeping your teeth, or it's not necessary.

My bet is that what your parents believed was instrumental in influencing and forming the habits you have now and as a result, you don't even think about them. To my point earlier, your brain wants to make anything that expends energy automatic!

Let's use this example and see how mindsets can be formed. You likely took on someone else's beliefs and thoughts about brushing and flossing and paired them with triggers (getting ready for bed or waking up) and actions and *Viola*! Over YEARS you created a habit.

Now this is key—the results you have in your mouth from brushing or not brushing, flossing or not flossing, are likely someone else's influence you adopted. You have a collection of beliefs, thoughts, feelings, actions, and triggers (a.k.a. a mindset) around brushing and flossing that ultimately gives you healthy or unhealthy oral hygiene. And what's more, you likely never think about how it came into being.

I can give you other easy examples. The health results you have in your life are a result of your habits around exercise, sleeping, eating, and taking care of yourself. How much you have saved in your bank or investment account is the return of your saving or not-saving habits. (There are always exceptions here; for example, if you received a windfall of money and your habits have not had time to impact that stockpile.) Rest assured that over time, your habits will catch up to you.

The results you have in your life can be a function of the beliefs and thoughts you have developed over time. Your outcomes can be tied to your habits and your habits can be tracked back to their influences. The mindsets you have and live out are automatic and likely a result of influences you had early on in your life. This is just one of the ways mindsets are formed.

Let's look at a few other ways. We can have natural defaults of thinking and believing if they aren't corrected by our parents. Communication is an example and usually has a direct tie to what was modeled for us growing up. There are traumas and experiences we have that form mindsets and beliefs. Gosh, there are all kinds of events that happen to us and ways relationships played out (see The Attachment Theory[10]) that develop deeply engrained ways of thinking and believing in our brains and our bodies' systems.

Let's explore a mindset that I have worked with a hundred times over the years that may just be a natural default, or maybe it needs very specific training. Most kids don't have the discipline to do something over time to see results. I know there are some of you who always came home and started your projects the day the teacher handed them out, and you are impressive. Anyway, understanding the consequences of starting to read a book the night before the book report is due doesn't always translate to developing a reading plan and sticking to it.

Most kids do their math homework because it is due the next day, but it doesn't mean they are learning how to manage a big project that is due in two weeks and needs to be worked on every day. My parents have a favorite story they tell from parents' weekend in college, when I nonchalantly mentioned I had a 25-page paper due in the next few days but hadn't started yet. Start something just in time to finish by the deadline. That was my way of operating.

It's possible that we've been influenced by our environments, people, and events as well as what we were and weren't taught. That said, many mindsets have developed because they lacked guidance or training. Our brains actually fill in the blanks to understand a story. We do this all the time and many times it leads to conflict. We fill in the missing information.[11] Kids do this by inserting themselves into the story; they decide or deduce, thinking that things that happen are because of them. "Mom left because of me," or, "Dad is always angry—it must be my fault." I knew a little girl who adopted a parent's ways of eating at an early age and landed in the hospital. When I delved in a little deeper to uncover her influences, she said something along the lines of, "Well one of my parents was doing this diet, and I just assumed I should do it too." My point here is that kids interpret the events of their lives through a filter that doesn't see the bigger picture. So, if you didn't have a parent constantly explaining to you why things happened, you created a story to fill in the blanks.

Before we go on, some of you parents may be unable to continue thinking about YOUR mindset because you're hung up on whether or not you have scarred your children. Let me insert something here. No parent does this perfectly, and it doesn't mean your child will be forever scarred. Yes, maybe you need to work on your mindset, and this will bring freedom to you. Then, you can model it for your own children, retrain and reparent them, or just share with them what you are learning.

You can change your mindsets if they are a hindrance to you and those around you, but you can't do it if you panic and take your focus off the work you need to do and put it onto others. I know you have heard the saying that most things kids learn are caught, not taught. Live out of a different mindset and trust me, your kids will feel it and maybe even get it because it's a new way of thinking, believing, acting, and ultimately talking.

Back to the point. This is just one of the ways you developed the mindsets that govern your way of operating. It's okay. It happens to all of us.

In a vacuum, kids (and adults) will make up a story because that is what our brains do. We fill in the blanks. Many times, beliefs about the way the world works, who we are, our identity, and our value come out of those stories. And unfortunately, they aren't often rooted in what is actually true.

But let's talk about you and your mindset and begin to explore how it formed.

If kids grow up trying to navigate their little emotional worlds, when they are scared or surprised or ashamed, they fill in the blank with a story, and beliefs likely form from that. Especially the things that happen consistently. Many times, they are just surviving in the absence of a constant someone to properly reframe the events in their lives.

Take a moment to ask yourself, what governs your life?

What overarching beliefs do you have?

This may be a little overwhelming initially but just try it on for a moment. Your mindset that helped you survive as a child, likely, is holding you back now in one way or another.

Were you a victim, so you filter everything through the lens of "things happen to me"?

Do you believe that life isn't fair?

Did you lose a parent when you were young and deduce you have no control over the events of your life? As a result, do you grip everything and every situation for control?

Were you treated unfairly, so you look for fairness and justice in everything?

Were you told you weren't the right size? Too tall, too short?

Do you now believe if you were more attractive, you would be more valuable?

Did you decide you weren't as valuable as the other kids, and there was something wrong with you? Leaving you feeling hopeless to change?

Did you have an alcoholic parent and never knew what you were walking into? You had to "read the room" to figure out how to avoid the landmines that might explode. Your safety and security depended on you reading every situation and assessing what you need to do to keep yourself and others safe.

What mindsets do you have and where did they come from?

Sidenote: Now would be a great time to start journaling if you haven't already.

Okay, so here is the thing: Kids are resilient. You were resilient. You made it through your childhood, and your mindset was your companion and way of thinking that helped you navigate the world!

Some of you did it all on your own. That little kid did the best they could with what they had. It's up to you, now, to let that little boy or girl off the hook. It's time for the adult to take over. The fact is that your younger self interpreted their world the only way they knew. And it's time to release them from their responsibility to get you through life. The mindset that developed to get them through life is likely not working for you now, especially if you are stuck in some way or area of your life.

Most of us are in the same boat—no one had perfect parents or perfect upbringings. Some of us were trained better than others toward healthier mindsets. For those who feel stuck in some way, even in small ways, I want to remove the mystery of why we are where we are. This isn't a black hole you are peering into that you can't figure out. I promise.

We needed teaching, training, building skills, receiving guidance, and putting boundaries in place FOR us. And many of us didn't get those things. So here we are. Here you are.

This book could be helpful to you for several reasons.

If you still can't crack the nut. Meaning, "I don't really understand why I'm stuck or why I do what I do."

Or if you feel hopeless to change. "I've been dealing with this my whole life. I feel frustrated and defeated because I can see there is a problem and yet can't fix it."

If any of these voices are in your head, you aren't alone and there is freedom!

About now, my friends and family can probably visualize me getting a little overly passionate, even annoyingly so. I start talking really fast and loudly when I get excited. But I believe people can change!

Where you are (notice I did not say WHO you are) in life is largely a function of the automatic mindsets that developed as you grew up and resulted in behaviors that produced certain results.

What am I saying? Your mindsets can be broken down into

different parts, and even summarized into a way of living and operating. The results you have in your life are a function of your mindset.

And now we are getting to the part I love! The hope of change is on the horizon!

If you are ready for something new, that's where we're headed.

7

You Have AGENCY!

T he bottom line is this: You don't have to change, but you can.

According to the *Open Education Sociology Dictionary*, **agency** is the capacity of an individual to actively and independently choose and to effect change; it is free will or self -determination.[12]

As an adult, you have agency!

Yes, you can change. You can make decisions to see clearly why you are where you are and to change directions.

You can release the childlike ways you learned to navigate your life. Identify and own the areas you want to grow in and take the responsibility to find a truer and better way of operating that will help you be the person you want to become or achieve the goals you want to reach.

You can release your younger you from their job of helping you make it in the world and invite them along on your journey. I read a book called *Big Magic* by Elizabeth Gilbert, and she said it this way: You invite fear (which she developed as a child) on the journey with you into the back seat. They are with you, but they don't get to give directions and they don't get to drive.[13] It is your turn to take care of them now in a way that maybe no one did. As the adult, you remake where you want to go and strategically make choices to get you there. And applaud the younger you that got you here because they did the best they could.

That agency you have now comes with the responsibility to do something with it. And there are two hurdles you will have to overcome in this process. The first is removing the mystery behind why you are stuck and the second is deciding you want to do something about it. Reading the principles and doing the work are totally different. You can know you are stuck and not do anything about it. *You will have to decide you want to change* and that doing the work is worth it. It isn't rocket science, but it does take time and a desire for something new and better.

In Part Two, you will see the principles of dissecting your old mindset into its parts clearly and in a way that will allow you to understand them differently. THEN you can rebuild it. I hope to remove the mystery of why you are stuck, and by doing that, give you hope you can change and move toward the life you want. Who doesn't want more intimate relationships, a deeper, richer, and more fulfilling life, and to live a life of purpose and meaning? I do and I think deep down, you do too.

8

We Always Have Choices

My old roommate, Emily Ruth, used to tell people that sometimes I take out my pen and paper or my journal in the middle of a movie to write down a quote or thought. I think one example was *Fireproof* with Kirk Cameron. Yes, I know, nerd alert. Not Kirk Cameron, me. But I learn so much from movies and TV! Listing a few characters who have profoundly impacted me and made it into my journal alongside Jesus and C.S. Lewis are Dumbledore, Ted Lasso, and Elizabeth McCord from *Madam Secretary*. I am so inspired, and true confession, I tear up when Ted Lasso lives out the words of Jesus in Luke 6:27-36, which talk about loving your enemies. "But to you who are listening I say: Love your enemies, do good to those who hate you, bless those who curse you, pray for those who mistreat you. If someone slaps you on one cheek, turn to them the other also. If someone takes your coat, do not withhold your shirt from them. Give to everyone who asks you, and if anyone takes what belongs to you, do not demand it back. Do to others as you would have them do to you.[14] I love how all of God's truths are ours no matter what.

Speaking of *Madam Secretary.* Something I learned from my BFF Téa Leoni and quote often, especially to my clients, is, *"I've never met a situation where I don't have a choice in the matter."*[15]

We all have the choice to stay where we are or to prioritize our progress, to work on it so we can move forward.

Surely, I am still stuck in some areas of my life. We all are. And as issues come up, we get to prioritize their importance in light of the other responsibilities we have. And decide to work on them.

I hope you are starting to believe you can change if you want to. It's impossible to be too far down the road to change the direction of your life. This is super exciting for you if you feel hopeless and like there's nothing you can do. You have choices. We always do.

Now a quick story to illustrate how mindsets run every area of our lives and why changing them can change everything.

9

It's Messy in the Middle

I was a slave to results. Angry at myself when I worked on something for a few days and didn't see the fruit I was expecting. I was in a pattern of trying to accomplish a certain thing and obsessing over seeing the results and rewards.

I had thoughts like, "I need to see that what I am doing is working." And I believed things like, "If I don't see results quickly, it's not working." I tried hard and looked for evidence of progress.

When there wasn't fruit in a few days or weeks, I believed a lie: What I'm doing doesn't lead to change. Flipping over to the other side of the coin, I quit. That thought developed into a belief: Nothing I do matters.

Feeling hopeless and out of control, I felt and believed I had no agency or control over myself or my life. The only fruit I produced was hatred at myself for not being able to change, and that led to finding ways to cope with my emotions.

Years after I had already made progress on my eating disorder, the All-or-Nothing Mindset was finally exposed. I saw the pervasiveness of that voice in my head in other areas of my life as well. It was always morphing and producing slightly different thoughts, but the same underlying beliefs were leading to the same feelings and fruit. Its presence was everywhere.

Building a new business.
   Putting together curriculum.
   Getting in shape.
   Living in the chaos of a remodel.
   Dating.
   Engagement.
   Wedding planning.
   And body image, where it originated.

When I started coaching. It took longer to build a practice than it did when I started counseling. I was frustrated. "Why is this so hard? Why don't people just trust me?" As I was trying a new avenue of helping people for free, I thought and then started to believe, "I can't even *give* my services away. Maybe I should just quit."

As I was living in my house during a full-scale remodel. "I hate being in the middle of this project. I hate all these decisions—I want to see what this is going to look like. I hate waiting, it's taking forever. I just want to be finished."

In my relationship that led to engagement and then marriage, I was gripped with fear. Journaling daily: fear, fear, and more fear. Questions like, "What is this going to look like, how will this go, what if this happens, what if I feel this way or he feels that way? I need to be able to see and know how this turns out. I hate the uncertainty of being in the middle."

In planning my wedding. I wanted to get to the day, to the end, to see how it was going to turn out. I needed to see and know things would go smoothly.

Now, I can see that all those things were offshoots of my All-or-Nothing Mindset, the same mindset that governed my eating issues. Needing to see the end, needing to see progress, needing to know with certainty that my investment would turn out the way I wanted. There was no room for trying and tweaking or doing something that didn't produce what I wanted. It was either trying and succeeding or, the flip side, quitting.

I still like the end though. The high of the day, the finished product. But now, I don't let myself get discouraged. When I start thinking my lack of results means my actions aren't producing fruit, I recognize it and stop and remind myself.

I don't make my actions today depend on what I see today. Where I am today will change over time, depending on my choices today.

Life isn't...
   All or nothing.
   Go big or go home.
   I failed so I am a failure.
   This person doesn't fit my perfect mold, so I need to break it off.

Nope, not at all.

If these things were true, I would have quit coaching, I would have hated the season of having my house remodeled instead of enjoying the process, and I would have given up on my relationship that ultimately led to marriage.

I still get stuck on things.

For example, I did not enjoy wedding planning. I could not get myself out of that mindset, but I did keep moving forward, which was a win. I made it to the day; I said yes, and I meant it. I stayed the course in spite of my scaredy-cat self, and I'm thrilled I did.

That voice, that stinkin' voice. I've quit so many things because they were hard or because I couldn't see they were producing the fruit I wanted. Now, I see. I see the Flawed Mindset. When it's governing me, I am stifled. I don't get things done, projects stall out, and I quit relationships or force things to work out when they need time to resolve.

But now I catch myself.

I realize everything and everyone grows over time. Change does not come overnight.

I've finally realized I must have faith and trust and believe that my actions produce fruit—sometimes good and sometimes bad, depending on what I nurture and how I choose to act.

Here's the thing. This is not a mystery.The All-or-Nothing Mindset is actually just a collection of parts, like every other mindset. It's no different than the mindset that has you stuck.

My Flawed Mindset begins with thoughts: "I have to know how this is going to turn out, if this investment is worth it, or else it's better to quit." It also begins with beliefs: "If I can't SEE progress, I must not be making any and I might as well quit." This leads to feelings like hopelessness, anger, and resentment. The accompanying actions are usually quitting a relationship, routine, book, or goal or always turning to the easier route that feels good. And don't forget the lagging fruit, stuck in the middle–not where I want to be but not trying anymore.

For years, I was single and wondering why I wasn't married. I had terrible frustrations with body image and slavery to food, not to mention the burden of living with half-completed projects and goals: photo albums, books read, and books written.

I've named my Mindset of Truth "Life Is a Journey."

For example, in my marriage to Curt. We are on a journey toward Heaven, together. Toward the same things, here to help each other as we move in that direction.

We aren't there. We haven't arrived. We aren't perfect. We are going to disappoint each other along the way. We both want to grow and honor God and yet it will be messy in the middle.

The middle is messy and THAT is life.

Before I discovered my mindset was at the root of much of my stuck-ness, I needed to see the end of the journey. I didn't have faith and I didn't TRUST.

The All-or-Nothing Mindset kept me from staying on ANY course of action, THROUGH the middle, and to the other side, where the harvest is.

I didn't love seeing things come together.
   I like the before and the after.
   I didn't like the middle.
   And this is how all mindsets work.

You have mindsets that keep you stuck. Your Scarcity Mindset(a mindset around money), your All-or-Nothing Mindset, and your Victim Mindset, to name a few.

And you have mindsets that cause you to thrive over time! An Abundance Mindset. Life Is a Journey. Generosity, and the list goes on!

We have mindsets that produce good fruit and mindsets that produce bad fruit. Your way of operating, or your mindset, is the culprit of the results you have in your life. But it's not that big and not that scary.

So, if you're stuck, it's not a mystery. It's just your mindset!

Now, through the middle to the other side, where the harvest is.

10

Emily's Story

How did you feel before starting the Link Program about the area you wanted to change?

I felt very frustrated. In some ways I knew what was wrong and couldn't fix it. In other ways, I had no idea where to start. I felt frustrated and lost.

Why was it important for you to try to do something different?

I was wanting something different in some areas of my life—mostly marriage. I knew it wasn't getting any better. What I had tried wasn't working and I knew the issue was deep inside me.

What was your experience with the Link Program?

I had a lot of realizations about thoughts and patterns I had developed over time. I had done a lot of work on myself before, but this helped me connect dots. It showed me how it all fit together. It got more to the root of why I was the way I was and then gave me some ways to start changing. Real action to start changing.

How did the program help you?

I changed! Patterns I had for years began to change. I started to have a peace about why things were the way they were and hope that they could be different. And they were! And are! I got unstuck in a few areas. Mainly related to anxiety that builds around certain situations and the desire/need to control them.

Did it help you accomplish your goals? If so, can you describe how?

Yes. It's hard to describe because a lot of it is feeling more at peace and comfortable with who I am. I'm closer to my husband in ways that are hard to describe. My relationship with the Lord has grown. I've grown in my ability to trust.

How did you feel afterward?

Enlightened. More at peace. More ok with the journey God has me on. Free.

II

Part 2

The four principles I wish I knew.

I know them now.

When I live by them, I chart a different course. Most of the time they are tiny changes. An ever so slight different trajectory.

And that trajectory ends in a crazy different place.

11

Hope for Change

Years ago, I really enjoyed teasing my parents about their new neighborhood. It was like a retirement community, and since they weren't very old, I think it sort of got their goat. The neighborhood was filled with older people who liked their yards just *so*. Naturally, my love for *Seinfeld* was rekindled. You are tracking with me if you are thinking about Jerry's parents' community in Florida.

One night when I was visiting, they told me about a neighbor-friend who measured her ground cover while her trusted yard man and his crew were working on the yard. Honestly, I assumed they were exaggerating a tad. The next morning, I walked into the kitchen and my dad said, "CC, come here quick." I walked to the window to see his neighbor out there with her yardstick just like they said, measuring her ground cover in different places to make sure it was even. I couldn't believe my eyes.

It took me a minute to shift from thinking like a junior high girl and put on my coaching hat, but I can see that *she* had a mindset about how she liked her yard, and quite possibly the things around her, even if it sucked all the joy out of her life. And for the record, if we knew her story, we would see she likely had very logical reasons for her actions. There is one saying I heard a long time ago and have found to be true: The things we do are not always rational, but they are always logical.

It pains me to see people walking around in a prison. So, whether you walk around your front beds and measure the ground cover, or like me, have other ways of operating that are robbing you of your life, I have the best news for you. You aren't stuck.

I'm not stuck, my parents' neighbor isn't stuck, and if you want something different, you're not stuck either. This is why I love helping people so much! I love the hope of this! You can change and there IS more! More life, more intimacy, more relationship, and more joy that God has for you. If you *can* change, then the bigger question is *how* you can change.

Let's start with where you might be today.

You want to change something in your life but either don't understand how because you have tried multiple things that haven't worked, or you don't see a clear pathway to the end goal you are wanting. Or you might just feel a whirlwind of control and dissatisfaction in your life.

I want to introduce the first of four key principles in this process as well as more fully develop the idea of "mindset" so you can grasp how they relate.

12

Principle One

Regarding where you are stuck, the root is a Flawed Mindset or way of thinking.

The Solution: Identify your Flawed Mindset and take it captive.

I n researching this topic, I came across a widely quoted line from the National Science Foundation. "It was found that the average person has about 12,000 to 60,000 thoughts per day. Of those thousands of thoughts, 80% were negative, and 95% were exactly the same repetitive thoughts as the day before."[16]

Whether or not these numbers are exact, it is safe to say we all have an inordinate number of thoughts per day. A large portion of those is subconscious, and according to the National Library of Medicine of cognitive behavioral therapy,[17] our thoughts, feelings, and behaviors are all closely connected. In the process of change, our first task is to gain an awareness of those thoughts. This brings me to our first principle.

Regarding where you are stuck, the root is a Flawed Mindset or way of thinking. The Solution? *Identify your Flawed Mindset and take it captive.*

Let's use my parents' neighbor-friend as a hypothetical scenario here since I have no idea what she was thinking. If she didn't like where she was in life and had no joy because she felt she had to control her surroundings, she may have been thinking something like, "I have to make sure they do this right; I have to be out there to ensure they do it the way I want it done. No one does things the way you want. If you want something done, you have to do it yourself. I feel anxious and worried they won't cut the yard all evenly and when I see it, the ground cover will be uneven. It must look 'this' way." Now moving to beliefs: "I can't be okay unless everything around me has order. Order has to be perfect order for me to feel okay. I can't be taken advantage of, and I am taken advantage of when people don't perform the exact service I want."

Now if you aren't a Bible person, don't worry, we are going to talk in neuroscience terms and, spoiler alert, you will see how they actually confirm one another.

When the Apostle Paul wrote one of his letters in the Bible to the Corinthian church, he included a behind-the-scenes look into his mind so that we could know that first, there is a battle over our thoughts, and second, how to fight it. 2 Corinthians 10:3-5 says, "For though we live in the world, we do not wage war as the world does. The weapons we fight with are not the weapons of the world. On the contrary, they have divine power to demolish strongholds. We demolish arguments and every pretension that sets itself up against the knowledge of God, and we take captive every thought to make it obedient to Christ."[18]

A pastor I have listened to, Matt Chandler, broke down this verse in a sermon. He says that the hurdle to being fully formed by the gospel is sin, and he nuances sin in terms of strongholds.[19] He goes on to say this about the New Testament: ". . .rarely when it talks about strongholds is it talking about demonic powers but rather broken mindsets."[20]

Another way I am defining mindset in this process is to mean a way of thinking, a thought process, a value system, or a set of deeply held beliefs that leads to certain feelings, actions, and resulting fruit. Over the next few chapters, we will be distinguishing between what I am calling the Flawed Mindset and the Mindset of Truth.

The Flawed Mindset is the way in which you are operating currently relating to the areas you want to change, and it often leaves you feeling stuck and frustrated. The Mindset of Truth is the way you operate when you are living the way you want to live, accomplishing your goals, or the way you need to live to change what you want to change.

As we discussed in Part One, many of our Flawed Mindsets developed early in life, and I want to underscore this next point, which is, we accept them as true. As a result, they fly under the radar and go unnoticed and unchallenged. Connecting back to Matt Chandler's previous quote about strongholds, ". . . we're believing something false."[21]

Think of your mindsets as a tree. Above the ground is what you see and notice: the branches, the fruit, and the flowers. These are your choices and the outcomes in your life, specifically for our purposes, the ones you have identified you don't like. Beneath the ground is the root system, the things that the fruit has grown out of; these are your thoughts and beliefs. Let me use a negative example from my own struggle with eating and body image to show you how this has worked.

I have struggled in this area for most of my life and actively battled it for over 24 years. However, only in the last five years have I realized that there has been a mindset governing my eating and body image struggle that I was completely unaware of. *It was the link I was missing leading to more consistent victory, which means more joy, more peace, less frustration, and less riding a rollercoaster.* The mindset was usually responsible for sabotaging my progress and governed many other areas of my life. It is the All-or-Nothing mentality, also known as black-and-white thinking. This, by the way, is a common mindset that keeps people stuck.

As I've shared, during most of my childhood and into adulthood, I studied the night before the test. I rarely started anything early or made small steps over time[22] to complete a project. It was usually "everything or nothing." This mindset governed school projects, studying, and tennis as well as body image, eating, and exercise, and it triggered serious frustration and self-hatred. Here is how the All-or-Nothing cycle worked in my eating and body image struggle. I looked for immediate results, the "All," and if I worked really hard at eating and exercising and didn't see them, I'd get angry that what I tried hadn't worked. I would then swing to the "Nothing" part of the cycle, which looked like throwing in the towel with exercise and turning to food for comfort, and self-hatred would follow. This all led to feelings of hopelessness and despair that I couldn't change and kept me in this cycle for decades.

What makes this a Flawed Mindset is that it isn't rooted in truth. It isn't true that because I don't see results in a week or two of hard work, I am not reaping results. But because of my mindset, I didn't see all that I wanted to see and gave up.

Wildly, I had worked on my eating and body image issues for 20 years, but I had not seen the All-or-Nothing Mindset as the core of so much of my frustration. As I uncovered the All-or-Nothing thinking, I began to see how it was one of the primary influences sabotaging my healthy cycle.

Correcting this mindset to what I call the Life Is a Journey Mindset has allowed me to accept the small changes over time[23] without going into the destructive cycle of anger and frustration. Uncovering these mindsets is your first step. Principle One says, **"Regarding where you are stuck, the root is a Flawed Mindset or way of thinking. Part of the solution is to first identify your Flawed Mindset and take it captive."**

While God introduces us to these principles in Scripture, they are also evident from the neuroscience perspective. Dr. Caroline Leaf writes, "That toxic thinking will change your brain wiring in a negative direction and throw your mind and body into stress."[24] This is a variation of what I am calling our flawed mindsets. I am defining those "flawed mindsets" for our purposes as choices, feelings, and the fruit of our actions that cause us to become stuck. It is difficult to change our behavior because the neural pathways in our brains are deep from years of repetitive thoughts.

As introduced in Part One, over time, our thoughts create these neural pathways in our brains, and the more we have entertained those thoughts, the deeper the pathways become. This works for us with healthy, productive thoughts and against us with unhelpful thoughts. Remember, our brains have ruts, like sledding down that hill of snow.[25] It is so much easier to sled down a path that is already carved out than it is to pave a new path for yourself. Likewise, it is difficult to change a thought pattern and subsequent actions to a new way of thinking and acting.

In the old pathway, you hop in at the top, the sled almost automatically slips right into the deep rut, and you slide down fast, easily, and with little effort. Creating a new pathway means picking up your sled, moving it over to a new spot, using your arms to push, and going more slowly down the hill with more effort. There is no rut there to slide into, so it takes more effort to pave a new way.

I always ask clients at the end of every coaching session what their takeaways are. The reason I do this is because reflecting on something is one way to learn. Meaning, to reflect on something and think about it is to dig out the rut. In her book, Dr. Leaf also states that "the deeper you think, the more you can change."[26]

Here are just two easy ways you can begin to think deeply: reflecting and journaling.

Before we move onto the next step, I want to give you some to-dos if you want to use this book as more than information and start working through these issues.

Exercise for you:

Spend 15 minutes journaling every morning. Journaling the answers to these questions: What are my literal thoughts related to the area I feel stuck in? What am I thinking about?

Write them down, unedited. The goal here is to record and capture the thoughts that are going through your mind so that we can begin to see how many of those have beliefs beneath them.

Journaling Question Prompts:
   What is the situation or area you are frustrated by or want to change? Write about it.

What are you thinking?

Write out your raw thoughts about the issue. Meaning, write out whatever is going through your brain related to this topic.

You will begin to see that your patterns of thinking have led to your core beliefs. In addition, the accompanying behavior patterns and choices you make as a result of those beliefs are responsible for causing you to be stuck. Seeing these choices is the first step to changing because you can't take ownership of your choices until you see them as just that. Choices.

As we go through this process, you will begin to see some of your patterns and the link between them and the current fruit in your life. Though you can't clearly see how everything relates, there should be hope for a different way.

After you have journaled for a few days, move to filling out the exercise below, taking your cues from the thoughts you've been recording.

Exercise for you:
   Begin to see your Flawed Mindset by filling out the categories below. Fill out the thoughts, beliefs, feelings, and subsequent categories. You can come back to the name and your overarching Flawed Mindset after you fill out the others. Look at the example following it if you have questions or get stuck.

If you want to download a formal copy from the Link Program coaching curriculum, you can go to https://cynthiabaker.co m/worksheets/ and click download on the Flawed Mindset Worksheet.

This is key! Don't let getting it right on this exercise keep you from moving forward. Guess what? That too is a mindset. Just start and jot down next to each category or on a separate sheet of paper what you are thinking.

Name
  Flawed Mindset
  Thoughts
  Beliefs
  Choices
  Results of Mindset
  Examples
  Big Picture Perspective
  Feelings
  Triggers

Example of a Flawed Mindset

Name

- Fran (Frantic)

Flawed Mindset

- Projects and procrastination

Thoughts

- I can't/don't want to work on that.
- I'll do it later. Ugh! There are so many things to do.
- I'm so frustrated with myself.
- I am sick of seeing that on my list.
- If I can't finish that now, I don't need to start.

Beliefs

- I can't feel okay unless these projects are completed.
- I can only feel good if the whole task is complete.

Choices

- Procrastination.
- Choose to do things that aren't really what I need to be doing so I can feel productive.
- Do nothing. Cope by watching TV or something else.

Fruit of Mindset

- Self-focus, self-absorbed.
- Frustration with myself.
- Seeing all the things I haven't done.
- A big project.

Examples

- A project that takes more than one sitting.
- Work projects—finishing workbook.
- Black and white, all or nothing.

Big Picture Perspective

- One failure/misstep ruins everything so I might as well quit.
- Angry, overwhelmed, stuck, anxious.

Feelings

· Frustrated, isolated, dread.

Triggers

· Setting aside hours to do something.
· Having a big project to do with no deadline.
· Something that is important but not urgent.
· No accountability.

Okay, it's time to transition to a coaching concept called "the positive anchor." This will set you up for Principle Two and uncover your Mindset of Truth.

13

Your Own Personal Anchor

My niece, Isabelle, was living in my home city of Dallas for the summer doing an internship, and I got used to talking to her regularly. On my walk one morning, I remember where I was when she called: the dead end at Oram Street, rounding the corner. I thought it was a little bit odd, 9:30ish. She should be starting her workday. Hmmm. I hope she's okay. I said, "Hi!" enthusiastically. She said "Hi!" In her little Izzy voice. She went on, "I have a situation."

Uhhh huh. I had a bad feeling. Maybe she was just calling for advice?

"I rescued these two puppies yesterday. Me and a friend were walking on the Katy Trail and. . ." You know how this story ends, so I'll fast forward.

Lucy is the sweetest dog! She looks like a Bernese Mountain Dog but has a much smaller stature. And I adore her. I am so thankful Isabelle jumped over a fence and went down into a ravine to rescue Hazel and Lucy, who we now know and love. Her pup and mine. They were tied to a tree in the Dallas summer heat and truly near death's door. Dr. Donaldson quickly let me know how sick they were when we took them to the vet, and I didn't think Lucy would make it through the day. I texted Curt a photo of Lucy with the words, "I want you to strongly consider letting us keep her." That sounds like a request to me. Since I had confirmed with Curt while we were dating how many dogs he was okay with us having (or me bringing home), I was feeling confident because I knew we were under our limit.

The rest is history.

In her first year, we were used to Lucy being sick—puny as we call it in my family. She had Parvo and some weird growth platelet issue on steroids. And of course, she gets carsick. Why wouldn't she? She's puny. Yes, this means she's thrown up between my seat and the console twice and then some. Once, on our trip to visit my parents in Tyler, Texas, about an hour and a half east of Dallas, I had Curt with me, so it was two against one.

When we got Tyler, of course, I was eager to get it cleaned up. This wasn't my first rodeo, so I immediately went for the paper towels, a plastic sack, and a handful of other things. Since it was my car and I have the curse of being both a neat freak and a clean freak, I was on a mission. Anyway, we went in and tended to Lucy and said hi to my parents. I just assumed Curt was following me out and would even lead the charge. Let me pause and mention that if I were wise (and I am sometimes not), I wouldn't dream of keeping score on things like helpfulness or thoughtfulness. But rationale and clear thinking didn't seem to register at that moment.

So, when 20 minutes into the cleanup Curt was nowhere to be found and my mom was bringing out the vacuum cleaner, I was fuming. "I mean, she can't help me," I thought. I wanted someone to help, or if I am really honest, do it for me! I wanted to be a very helpful assistant. Seriously, cleaning in between the seats and the console is maddening. And right about the time I was finished and had worked myself up into a complete tizzy, mad as a hornet, Curt waltzed out into the driveway in a Ted Lasso sort of way. How could he possibly not realize that I was cleaning up the vomit while he was chit-chatting with my dad and watching the dog? HOW could he be that obtuse? Being newly married, I was trying to learn to communicate differently than my natural tendency. Quiet, withdrawn, no eye contact, evil eyes—all the things including marching around like a martyr, letting him subtlety figure out I was mad.

I think the Holy Spirit exploded in my body and took over my angry lizard brain. In the calmest and sweetest voice, I had one of the greatest moments thus far in my life handling my anger in a productive way. I said something like, "Hey, I'm just frustrated that I was out here cleaning the car and you weren't here to help me." Zero surprise, he responded in the sweetest, most non-defensive way. "Oh gosh, I am so sorry. I was out there with your dad and finally realized that you were probably out here cleaning, so I jumped up to come help." Of course, you did. Thanks, Ted.

The point of the story is that THIS is my positive anchor! I always go back to this memory. It is how I want to handle conflict when I'm angry and operating in my Mindset of Truth. When I am breathing fire about something, my normal flawed way of handling things is silent but fuming, avoiding eye contact but smoke seeping out of my ears. In contrast to when I am in my Mindset of Truth, I communicate my feelings honestly and in the moment. "I'm frustrated about this," in a normal voice, believing the best about the other person and giving them the chance to tell me their side of the story.

For you, a positive anchor is a time, a moment, or a situation when you thought, felt, believed, or acted how you want to do things when you are living out your goal the way you want to live it out.

Now that you have spent some time journaling and getting familiar with your Flawed Mindset, we are working toward a glimpse into your Mindset of Truth. You will find this by finding your positive anchor. Identifying the Flawed Mindset is often the hardest part of the process because up to now, it has been part of you. Now, you are separating from it and seeing it as a way of operating, not as a definition of who you are.

As I have mentioned, coaching is first about discovering the things you don't know so that you can have awareness in the moment and ultimately make different choices.[27] So, the steps are Discovery, Awareness, and Choices.[28] Discovering the Flawed Mindset is step one. That allows you to begin step two, which is becoming aware in the moment. As you become aware in the moment, you will probably think something like, "Great— now what do I do with this?" Don't worry; that question will be answered!

This next section is devoted to helping you figure out where to go from there. But before we do that, I want to give you a chance to find your own positive anchor. After that, we are going to uncover what I call the Mindset of Truth. I like to say that the Mindset of Truth involves you living out who God made you to be and responding to things in the way in which you feel a sense of peace and joy.

This next exercise will help you begin to till up the soil around your Mindset of Truth by discovering how you think and feel and what choices you make when you are operating in your sweet spot, that place you feel a sense of freedom and peace about life.

Now it's your turn. I want you to identify a time, moment, or event in your mind. Write where you were functioning in that sweet spot. Identify certain moments, seasons, or events when you were doing the things that you are trying to move toward—a.k.a. your goals. The more situations you can identify, the better. Again, nothing about this process is rigid. You are gathering data and information and making sense of it right now. If you can think of examples as well as how you are living when you are being the person God made you to be (if you are a Christian, you can think of it in terms of operating in the Spirit), then draw on all of those as examples as you begin to explore your Mindset of Truth in the next section.

Exercise for you: **Answer the following questions to flush out your own personal positive anchor. If you want to download a formal copy from the Link Program coaching curriculum, you can go to https://cynthiabaker.com/worksheets/ and click download on the Positive Anchor Worksheet.**

What were you doing or what was happening? (e.g., being true to yourself, standing up for yourself or someone else, being courageous and stepping into the fear that holds you back)

What were the values you were living out? (e.g., adventure, integrity, peace, freedom)

How did you feel?

What thoughts and beliefs did you have that made you feel hopeful?

What was your perspective?

How were you seeing life?

What was significant about this event/time to you?

Okay, it's time to take what you know about your own way of doing things when you are successful and rebuild the way you operate! It's the key to making this shift.

14

Lynn's Story

I am grateful to my clients for allowing me to share their stories. Lynn's story will help you see the next principle in action before you read it. Consider rereading her story after you read Chapter 11 to further see how to discover what is "more true" and how it is the key to your freedom.

Let me introduce you to Lynn. She was confused, living with dread, stressed, anxious, and fearful when we started coaching. Her *Flawed Mindset* was marked by thoughts and beliefs like, "This is too hard," "I don't know how to do it," "I am confused, afraid of failing." Lynn was operating in an All-or-Nothing Mindset.

Over the course of coaching, she learned how shift into her *Mindset of Truth* which left her joyful, grateful, curious, positive, and hopeful. Her *Mindset of Truth* is marked by a new philosophy: "I can't leap across an entire river, but I can look for the next rock to step on. I am moving in the right direction. Confidence develops through doing. I don't have to prove anything."

Lynn was able to identify the root of some problematic behaviors that were hindering her in her life and job. She was able to develop a new mindset to address those problem areas. Before coaching, she had experienced moments of this mindset but now she was able to articulate it more clearly and develop the skills to consciously shift into it.

This process left Lynn feeling empowered and hopeful about how both her life and work could change. In her words, she recounts this.

When I started: I didn't realize why I was often coming across with too much intensity, or how to change that other than just shutting down.

Now: I knew that I'm a verbal processor, but now I understand that I also crave external validation in order to shore up a fragile sense of self. The Mindset of Truth I've been working on helps me recognize that I don't need to prove or earn my value. What is more true is that listening well is a way to show love to others as well as learn, and that is what I desire more than to attempt to impress others.

When I started: I had a fear of inadequacy that led me to avoid hard things. I had a belief that "other people know how to do that. I don't know how to do that."

Now: I understand that the unknown is a place I can explore. I don't know how long it will take or exactly what the path is, but that exploration is part of the process. If I have patience and persistence, I will develop the skills I need to be successful.

When I started: I was somewhat aware of my Flawed Mindset, but much less aware of what a "Mindset of Truth" could look like. I had simplified it to focusing on the positive, focusing on gratitude, taking a deep breath, and trusting God. While these are good practices, they weren't specific enough to address the places where I was stuck.

Now: Probing deeper into the Flawed Mindset and getting specific about "What is more true?" has helped me uncover some strategies to address the places where I was stuck.

In order to continue the growth that has begun, I will continue to ask myself, "What's the smallest step I can take in the right direction?" when I feel stuck. I will journal my answers to the question, "What is more true?" And I will lean into developing new skills and pushing past the fear and impatience I feel in the process.

15

Principle Two

Your freedom depends on your focus.

<u>The Solution</u>: Build and develop a new narrative on which to focus your mind.

On Friday mornings, my husband and I do what we call "coffee talk." The Thompsons, who performed our wedding ceremony and have been counseling couples for years, recommended this to us as a way to connect with each other. A weekly coffee. All the things I love, together. I can do that.

One Friday during our weekly coffee talk chat, I had a breakthrough. Let me back up for a moment. This past year I have had a mindset that has needed serious rewiring. Suffice it to say I have been ruled by fear. Through a year of neck problems including MRIs, Xrays, doctor visits, and now finally physical therapy, I've resigned myself strictly to walking and dance class for exercise. My PTs have all said that people with neck trouble have a mental hill to climb in addition to the physical part. There is some fear with neck problems that is different from other body parts.

On that Friday, my breakthrough was this: I don't have to resign myself to being fragile and fearful. I don't have to live like this. Fear has been keeping me from pursuing the next steps that I need to take and has even been my companion on a few normal daily activities. But on that day in just one moment, I had hope.

What happened was something that you are going to learn how to do intentionally. What do I mean by that?

You don't have to see things the way they have been. You can shift the way you see your circumstances by shifting what you focus on. How you do this leads me to the next principle and solution. *Your freedom depends on your focus.* The Solution? *Build and develop a new narrative on which to focus your mind.*

Principle Two involves renewing our minds specifically to what is true; in other words, rebuilding our thoughts to specific truths by building and developing a new narrative on which to focus our minds.

In Romans 12:2 Paul says, "Do not conform to the pattern of this world but be transformed by the renewing of your mind."[29] The word "renew" is defined in one way as rebuilding or replacing.[30]

Our focus is important because of those ruts in our brains and here is the key. *Our focus determines which rut on our snow-covered trail we slide down.*

Our focus is the key to determining which path we choose.

Dr. Caroline Leaf says it this way, "It is our choice to pay attention that influences this internal chatter in a positive or negative direction."[31]

Here is the awesome news: We get to choose our focus and therefore our path! You can reframe your old destructive thoughts to life-giving truths.

I don't have to focus on, brood over, or zero in on the way of thinking in which I have been stuck. I can purposefully and intentionally develop a new narrative to refocus my mind and actually place my thoughts on what I want to achieve.

Paul says it this way in Philippians 4:8. "Finally, believers, whatever is true, whatever is honorable and worthy of respect, whatever is right and confirmed by God's word, whatever is pure and wholesome, whatever is lovely and brings peace, whatever is admirable and of good repute; if there is any excellence, if there is anything worthy of praise, think continually on these things [center your mind on them, and implant them in your heart]."[32]

Many Christians often meditate on this verse, but the verse tells us to think about "these things." What are "these things" he is talking about? They are "whatever" is true, honorable, right, and wholesome—specifically. We stop short when we do not take the step to name them specifically. I like to approach this principle by asking you to answer the question, "What is *more* true?" Often, we are focused on partial truths or pat answers, and those become the whole truth. Let me give you some examples.

A destructive and limiting thought or belief sounds like this: "What if my neck isn't stable? They aren't going to figure out what is wrong and I'm going to be in pain and have to live with these limitations forever. What's going to happen if I get in a car wreck, or I fall? I can't do anything plus I am scared of all the possible outcomes."

A pat answer to try to overcome that destructive thought sounds something like this: "I can't do anything about it, so I just need to get over it and move forward. I may have to give up a few hobbies but I'm sure I'll be okay."

The new narrative and what is *more* true (a.k.a. a bigger picture) sounds like this: "I don't have to live in fear of what could happen. Yes, I could fall or get into an accident, but I could also get attacked by coyotes while out walking. I do have to trust the Lord with the outcomes, and I can move forward toward some of the procedures that could help me even though they scare me. I have to keep living my life. My physical therapist says that people with neck issues do have fear of these things so I have to rewire my brain to trust that things are currently stable and do the work of changing the things I can."

Okay, so you probably don't relate to all that, which is great. The point of the examples is to help you see this. When you are painting a new narrative, it is necessary to name the "whatever" in your specific circumstances. There are 100 different ways to reframe any given thought, and we have to do the work to reexamine them. We have to say what is true, and we have to create a new narrative that is just as strong as the one we are currently fighting.

I think we believe the destructive things because we can be a little lazy and because they usually have a hint of truth. We look at them and say, "Well it's true," excusing ourselves to stay in self-sabotaging thoughts. But again, we get to choose our focus and therefore our path!

Principle Two is rooted in neuroplasticity, which we discussed in Part One. It's defined by the *APA Dictionary of Psychology* as, "the ability of the nervous system to change in response to experience or environmental stimulation."[33] *Psychology Today* says it this way: "Neuroplasticity is the brain's capacity to continue growing and evolving in response to life experiences. Plasticity is the capacity to be shaped, molded, or altered; neuroplasticity, then, is the ability for the brain to adapt or change over time, by creating new neurons and building new networks."[34]

The point is this: Our brain is always changing, and this includes the ability to create new ways of thinking.

As I mentioned earlier, according to Dr. Leaf, "It can operate for us as well as against us, because whatever we think about the most will grow."[35]

The more you reflect on the thoughts you take captive and reframe or rebuild them, the deeper your new neural pathway becomes. Developing a new neural pathway and deepening that rut in your brain is equivalent to changing the way your brain thinks. And when you change that, you change everything.

Now is the time to pick up your sled, march to the other side of the mountain, and begin to slide down. And do it again and again and again. I love this quote: "When a person is focused on something, they're paying attention to it. When a camera lens or your eyes are focused, they've made the adjustments needed to see clearly." As you change your focus, you make adjustments to see clearly.[36] Seeing things clearly or truthfully allows you to change the choices you make and thus the fruit you have.

I think this is one of the most exciting parts of the process but is often hard for people because it is where we begin to learn how to think differently. If you look at the thoughts and beliefs of your Flawed Mindset, you might see thoughts you have nursed for years.

Now it's time to rebuild them and create a new narrative. The old ones are ingrained, so you will need to take some time to think about the new truths. A pat answer isn't usually enough thought. It can be part of the "*more* true", just not all of it. You need to do the work to "think." Again, that is one way you begin to carve out new ruts.

I frequently hear clients say, "I don't know how to reframe this," or, "I don't think I am doing it right." Please don't take offense to this, but these are often smoke screens for what they actually mean: "This activity is hard and takes some thought."

Yes, it is, and yes, it does. Remember, when you are thinking hard about things, you are digging out your new rut and sledding down your new trail. The more you think, the better. The harder you think, the better. That is part of the process of change!

Thinking is part of the healing process. It is hard, but more than that, it is different from what you are used to doing. Once you begin to shift and see this new way of thinking, it is just a matter of practice.

16

Principle Three

Part of the power and blessing is in the doing.

<u>The Solution:</u> **Practice and live out your new narrative.**

There is a "doing" piece to this formula that is embedded in God's economy. Knowing a truth in your head is not what makes it real in your life. Our action, mysteriously, is a part of the equation. For the longest time, I wanted knowing the truth and thinking about it, sort of like a reminder, to be enough. After all, the book of Romans instructs us to be transformed or changed by renewing our minds.

I have come to understand something very different: This equation is incomplete. When I realized this, I became more hopeful. I had never practiced what the Scriptures exhort us to do. I resisted the discipline I had heard so much about because I knew it would be hard and, to be honest, I didn't like using those muscles. Now, I am getting the fuller picture and I see it everywhere, which leads me to Principle Three. **Part of the** *power and blessing is in the doing.* The Solution? *Practice and live out your new narrative.*

Generally speaking, in God's economy there is required action on our part. Of course, I would never go to the extreme and say that God doesn't do miraculous works without our effort; clearly, He does! But in John 13:17 (the night Jesus was arrested), He said to the disciples, I just washed your feet, and you should do this too. (I am paraphrasing of course.)

Okay, so that's not new news for many of you! I knew he said that, but my jaw dropped when I read John 13:14-17 in the Amplified version. "So if I, the Lord and the Teacher, washed your feet, you ought to wash one another's feet as well. For I gave you [this as] an example, so that you should do [in turn] as I did to you. I assure you and most solemnly say to you, a slave is not greater than his master, nor is one who is sent greater than the one who sent him. If you know these things, you are blessed [happy and favored by God] if you put them into practice [and faithfully do them]."37

Another translation says, "If you know these things, blessed and happy and to be envied are you if you practice them (if you act accordingly and really do them)."38 You are happy and blessed if you practice and really do them?! Of course, intuitively, I know that it isn't enough to just believe I should serve others but seeing in writing that the blessing and happiness occur as we faithfully do something was so revolutionary. Why, I am not sure, but I always thought that the primary way I could be changed was by renewing my mind. In theory, this strategy is nice because it doesn't require much beyond the work I do on my mind. Renewing your mind is part of the equation, but it isn't the whole equation. Now, it should be noted here that Jesus is specifically referring to "washing others' feet" (serving others) as the way to blessing and happiness. We aren't making a theology of change out of that one passage.

In Philippians 4:9, Paul says, "Practice what you have learned and received and heard and seen in me, and model your way of living on it, and the God of peace (of [e]untroubled, undisturbed well-being) will be with you."[39] Another version says it this way, "The things which you have learned and received and heard and seen in me, practice these things [in daily life], and the God [who is the source] of peace and well-being will be with you."[40] And I am assuming that when the God of peace and well-being is with you, you have His peace.

Okay now for neuroscience. This blew me away!! According to Dr. Leaf's fifth step in her process called Active Reach, she says, "You can be presented with all the reason, logic, scientific evidence, and just plain common sense in the world, but you won't believe something is true unless your brain's limbic system—the central location of your emotions—allows you to feel that it is true."[41] She says that the action *"helps you feel whether or not something is true."*[42]

Back to Jesus' exhortation in John. We will be happy and blessed when we "do" these things. Our actions actually allow us to feel that things are true,[43] which in turn changes our beliefs. What?! There is a link between our beliefs and our actions because then the action is also part of what deepens the new ruts and allows it to stick.

Your thoughts lead to feelings which lead to actions and the other way around as well. They can all influence one another.[44] In my experience, one of the fastest ways to get back on track to your Mindset of Truth is through performing an action. When I do something in accordance with my Mindset of Truth, my brain responds, my thinking responds, and my feelings respond. They are all linked together.

Renewing your mind equals thinking. Practicing equals doing. Yes, there are two parts. Renewing your mind with what is *more* true is one, and practicing it or doing something with it is the second part.

This is not behavior modification because we have already done what the late Tim Keller said we have to do to change, which is dig down into our thinking.[45] One day, my friend and fellow coach Emily and I were breaking this principle down in relation to my own eating and body image issues. We discussed that when I am making choices in keeping with the changes I want to make, and even if the old path isn't where I necessarily am anymore, an event can elicit feelings that drop me right back into that old cycle. Emily added that having a thought that's congruent with your old way of thinking or your old path does not mean you have to go right back there and continue on the old path. You can simply focus on what's true, think about how to respond in the new way of thinking, and get back on the new path.

This is where people get stuck and off their new path. Our feelings are just reactions to something but can trigger us back to the old cycle. In and of themselves they are powerless, though they can feel debilitating. How we respond to them can determine which hill or path we slide down. If we act in accordance with the old way, we begin to slide down the old pathway and open those old ruts.

This part is worth doing cartwheels over! We can consciously make choices in keeping with the new path of blessing and peace we are on even if we don't feel like it. We don't have to go back to the old path.

I want to end this principle with the story of Moses and Joshua written in Exodus 17:9-14. "Moses said to Joshua, 'Choose some of our men and go out to fight the Amalekites. Tomorrow I will stand on top of the hill with the staff of God in my hands.' So Joshua fought the Amalekites as Moses had ordered, and Moses, Aaron and Hur went to the top of the hill. As long as Moses held up his hands, the Israelites were winning, but whenever he lowered his hands, the Amalekites were winning. When Moses' hands grew tired, they took a stone and put it under him and he sat on it. Aaron and Hur held his hands up—one on one side, one on the other—so that his hands remained steady till sunset. So Joshua overcame the Amalekite army with the sword. Then the Lord said to Moses, 'Write this on a scroll as something to be remembered and make sure that Joshua hears it, because I will completely blot out the name of Amalek from under heaven.'"[46]

The story shows us so many things. First, God is the One behind the scenes giving the victory. He is the agent of change, and yet in His ways and in how He created our world to work, we participate with Him (not in salvation of course). When we partner with Him, something supernatural happens with our actions. It is a mystery, but He uses it to bring about victory in our lives and the lives of others.

We can even see this in the example of Moses. The work was hard, even grueling at times, and he needed a friend on each side of him to achieve the victory. He couldn't do it alone, without God or without His people. There is a partnership of some kind with God, a mysterious link between His power and our action. One friend said, "He uses our obedience to change us."

Let me say it this way: our participation is evidence of our faith that He can heal and change us. And that healing doesn't usually bear total freedom in that moment. He works in seeds. Us planting, sowing, and watering and Him bearing the fruit. A partnership.

This is true even in areas of our lives that have wounding and trauma-related tentacles. We still have to show up. God has to sew up the wound in a supernatural way that only He can do, but this truth is not mutually exclusive from us doing our work. He can "touch" us and totally and completely heal us. It just isn't how He usually works. He wants us to participate and trust Him with the results.

Before we go onto the last principle, it's time to use your positive anchor to begin to capture your Mindset of Truth.

Look at the example following this next exercise to get a feel for it and start filling out your own thoughts, feelings, actions and all the other categories. You may want to come back to the name and mindset of truth after you have completed the other categories. Use your positive anchor to help you see how you are operating when you are operating the way you want to be. You've got this! **And if you want to download a formal copy from the Link Program coaching curriculum, you can go to https://cynthiabaker.com/worksheets/ and click download on the Mindset of Truth Worksheet.**

Exercise for you: Mindset of Truth

Name
  Mindset of Truth
  Thoughts
  Beliefs
  Choices
  Results of Mindset
  Examples
  Big Picture Perspective
  Feelings
  Triggers

Example of a Mindset of Truth

Name

- Bobbie (Bubbly, Open, and Brave)

Mindset of Truth

- Small steps over time will get me where I want to go.

Thoughts

- I can knock that out pretty quickly.
- I am excited to do that task and check it off.
- I feel so great to keep moving and making progress.
- I am getting good at doing small steps over time.

Beliefs

- I feel good when I make progress.
- I don't have to be finished with the task.
- Break out a project into small tasks.

Choices

- Do one of the tasks every day (to keep momentum).
- Start. Just do one small thing.
- Just spend 10 minutes to get started. Example: print a document and just review it.
- Feel free.

Fruit of Mindset

- Feel confident in my ability to get things done.
- I see projects as challenges to break down and start on.
- Completing a big project.

Examples

- A small project that feels hard for some reason.
- One step off my plan won't kill me.

- Make small changes over time.

Big Picture Perspective

- The Journey Mindset–Life is a journey.
- I am going to make mistakes and that means I am growing and risking new things, which is ultimately good.
- It's an opportunity to learn and grow.
- Hopeful, free, confident.

Feelings

- Joyous, energized, open.

Triggers

- Writing down a project and breaking it down into small tasks I can do one or two of per day.
- Selecting one or two tasks from a project to complete each day over the course of a week.
- Having a deadline.
- Scheduling an appointment to create a deadline.

17

Principle Four

Practicing your new narrative daily will lead to blessing—OVER TIME.

<u>The Solution</u>: Practice over time no matter how you feel.

This is by far my favorite principle. It was the principle that changed my life forever.

In Bambara, the language spoken in Mali, West Africa, there is a saying: *Dooni dooni kono ni be so dilan.* It means, "Little by little, the bird builds its nest." Our American culture seeks the opposite. We want instant success, for our videos to go viral on the first post, weight loss in a week, and mastery of a hobby immediately without having to put in the work that makes for true mastery of a subject. It's just human nature. If given the choice, would you rather something come easily to you or have to work for it?

Really? What a ridiculous question. Of course, most of us want ease, but the reality is that isn't how mastery, achievement, and success usually find their way into our lives.

Before he took on the role of Hannibal Lecter, for which he received an Academy Award, Anthony Hopkins acted in a crazy number of musicals on Broadway over the course of many years. In the book *Grit,* Angela Duckworth makes this point, "We want to believe that [Olympic swimmer] Mark Spitz was born to swim in a way that none of us were and that none of us could. We don't want to sit on the pool deck and watch him progress from amateur to expert. We prefer our excellence fully formed. We prefer mystery to mundanity."[47] Meaning, we don't like the idea of doing mundane tasks in our craft to become great. We prefer to believe in talent as the magic key unlocking the door to greatness. But the reality is that even Michael Phelps, who was built to swim, was successful because of both his natural talent and his thousands of hours of practice.

I have come to believe and feel insulted on behalf of extremely successful people when we say they got there because of talent. To be sure, talent may have gotten Michael Phelps there sooner than others, but if he never stepped foot in a pool, he would never have become a swimmer. And if he never became a swimmer, he never would have become an Olympic legend. Those choices didn't just happen. They happened because he dedicated himself to swimming and no one, not even someone with a six-foot-seven-inch wingspan, achieves their highest dreams without working for them.

The book *Grit* by Angela Duckworth along with *The Compound Effect* by Darren Hardy changed my life about 10 years ago. As the girl who did the night-before-the-test kind of studying in all areas of my life, these two books together changed my belief system. It went from "These people are different," to "These people worked so hard, and they deserve to be where they are." It changed my belief system to believe that success doesn't come overnight on the first go, nor should it.

Many of the people I coach are stuck because they had so much talent as kids that they never had to learn how to work hard. Getting through hard things wasn't something they had done, let alone mastered. But if you talk to people who have done really great things, you will find somewhere in their story, they attended the School of Hard Things.

I read the book *Fearless Leadership* by Carey Lohrenz a few years ago. Carey's dream was to be a naval aviator in a time when women were prohibited from flying combat aircraft. Undeterred, she enlisted and then endured the grueling training required. When the Department of Defense finally lifted the "Combat Exclusion Clause" allowing women to fly combat jets, she was ready.[48] She went on to become the first woman to fly an F-14 Tomcat. As she tells her story, one of the many parts that brought me to tears was the story of her as a baby. She was born with hips that weren't fully formed and underwent surgery ultimately to be placed into a half-body cast, crawling and dragging it around for nearly the first two years of her life.[49] There it was again. The difficult circumstances in life producing the ability to endure hard things.

She endured HARD things early in life and learned, even as a baby, how to push through them. When she talked about her training for flight school, I marveled as she described some burn in her lungs and calves that I had never experienced. Even as a runner and marathoner (recently turned walker), I have never pushed my body to that point. I can't begin to know what it is like to endure that kind of pain and push past it. Her long-term success was tied to her grit and her perseverance. Both are part of Principle Four. Success comes over time.

Carey Lohrenz, Anthony Hopkins, and Michael Phelps all worked on their crafts over time, in fact, over a lifetime. Looking into these seemingly untouchable people, I have found a work ethic in their stories that each included the "over time" principle.

No success is achieved overnight.

My belief system finally changed when I realized that people's success was first and foremost because they had worked hard. Yes, it's my hope that we can have most of the successes we are willing to put our effort toward, but I have in fact aged out of becoming an astronaut, and you likely have aged out of some of your dreams too. (To be clear, I never wanted to be an astronaut, but hopefully, you are picking up what I am putting down.) Although my belief system has changed to "It takes work over time to achieve a goal," that doesn't mean I can do anything in the world. We have limitations and that's okay. In fact, it's life. And onward we go!

Over the years, I have heard that it takes 21 days to create a new habit. But Health Transformer's web article "The Neuro-science of Behavior Change" says, "In terms of repetition, it is estimated that it takes 10,000 repetitions to master a skill and develop the associated neural pathway. It is estimated that it takes 3-6 months for a new behavior to become a habit, though this estimate varies by person. As clinicians, we can encourage patients that, with time, their repetition will pay off when their behavior becomes natural."[50]

The same article later quotes Psychologist Deann Ware, Ph.D., and explains that ". . .when brain cells communicate frequently, the connection between them strengthens and 'the messages that travel the same pathway in the brain over and over begin to transmit faster and faster.' With enough repetition, these behaviors become automatic. Reading, driving, and riding a bike are examples of complicated behaviors that we do automatically because neural pathways have formed."[51]

The fourth and last principle is, *Practicing your new narrative daily will lead to blessing—OVER TIME.* The Solution? *Practice over time no matter how you feel.*

This is so important because I believe it is a place where many people fall off the wagon. The All-or-Nothing thinking can easily derail a person who thinks they have done something for a few weeks, haven't seen the results they are looking for and quit.

That was my tendency. How many of us would plant one seed and expect a harvest? But I have to admit that I will try something once or twice, and if I am really diligent, for a week or two, and if it doesn't work or I don't see the results I want, I assume it didn't work, and consequently quit.

Remember in Part One when we talked about sowing and reaping? Here it is. In Galatians 6:7-9, Paul says, "Do not be deceived: God cannot be mocked. A man reaps what he sows. Whoever sows to please their flesh, from the flesh will reap destruction; whoever sows to please the Spirit, from the Spirit will reap eternal life. Let us not become weary in doing good, for at the proper time we will reap a harvest if we do not give up."[52]

There is no getting around the idea that God has placed the law of sowing and reaping into our world, and sowing and reaping are ongoing actions. Just to review the Scriptures we looked at in Principle Three, Philippians 4:9 said, "practice these things [in daily life],"[53] and in John 13:17 Jesus said you will be happy and blessed "if you put them into practice [and faithfully do them]."[54] Is it starting to make sense? In John, Jesus is saying that you can know these things, but both the peace of God and the blessing come as you practice these ways. They are inseparably linked.

This principle has to be part of your plan and what you will need to do to succeed. As you develop a plan of small action steps, examine it in light of filling in the gaps between where you are now and where you want to be.

Guess what? That's it. It is NOT that big and NOT that scary. It is just your mindset. You are not your thoughts! Or let me say that differently. You can control the thoughts and narrative you dwell on and therefore ultimately your feelings and how you choose to act, finally over time getting different results.

You have finished exploring four principles of making lasting change. Next in Part Three, we are going to summarize these principles into a step-by-step process that you can walk through.

III

Part 3

The steps aren't hard, they just take effort.
And all important things takes effort.

Your life is wildly important.

18

Four Principles and Ten Steps

U p to now, you may have felt confused about why you have the results you have, unable to connect the dots between why you are where you are and where you want to be. You can see there is a problem but haven't been able to understand why you're stuck doing the same thing over and over. You may even feel hopeless because you have been dealing with this for a long time and are teetering with being resigned to staying where you are.

By now, I hope you see there is a way out. If that is all you see, and you don't see how to do it for yourself, that's okay! It's taken me years and I still have work to do. Having the hope that there is a way to change is the very first thing you need.

One of the things I want to answer here is why I think this process of mindset work is different from other ways of changing. It is by no means the only way to effect lasting change. It is just one way, but I think it has four critical elements that all change must have to become permanent. These are the four principles discussed in Part Two, but don't worry—they are woven into the Ten Steps in this section.

In this last section, I am going to lay out the Ten Steps to guide you through the mindset shift process. Now is probably a good time to introduce the law of getting out of something what you put into it. And there is no shame here! I just want you to know without a doubt that you can change and it's worth putting in the work.

If you want to go deeper at the end of the book, I'll point you to my coaching content. The Link Program is a more in-depth process that takes you step by step through specific exercises, helping you get where you want to go. (For more information, you can click on linklifecoaching.com)

Before we move into the Ten Steps, I want to reiterate the four principles illustrating why I think people stay stuck and why it matters. As a coach, when I think of the things that I work on and why people stay where they are, these are four common themes I see in each principle.

Principle One: People stay where they are because they aren't aware of the thoughts and beliefs underneath the areas where they are stuck. This matters because our thoughts and beliefs usually drive our feelings, actions, and the fruit of our behavior.

Principle Two: People generally don't take the time to uncover, let alone rewire, the beliefs that govern their minds to some-thing that is true. This matters because if we don't have a clearly defined and built-out way of thinking about a topic or issue, we don't have other thoughts and beliefs to fall back on. We can't just change our behavior without a new way of thinking to accompany it and sustain the changes. Otherwise, our old thoughts will eventually interrupt and lead to the same old feelings, actions, and yes, results.

Principle Three: People don't act on their new beliefs, so they don't feel true. And since they don't feel true, they stop acting on them, falling back into the same cycle of old behavior. This matters because acting on new thoughts and beliefs is what makes a new belief feel like it's true, according to Dr. Leaf.[55] If you are trying to institute new ways of living to support a different life you want, you have to do different things and do things differently. The feeling of confidence comes after we have done something over time. We can act confidently, but the feeling and belief come after we have had enough repetitions to begin to believe it is true.

Principle Four: People don't act long enough on their new beliefs to give themselves time to see results, and therefore, quit too soon. This matters because very few goals are achieved in one sitting. Everything, including people, grows over time. It takes time to work on something to produce results. Many of us quit before the harvest.

Okay, those are my reasons people stay stuck.

But not you!

19

Break It Down

Steps 1-5

I n this next section, I will break the process down into steps for you. As you connect the dots and get to the root of why you are stuck, my hope is you will find the motivation to make the changes you need to make. As you begin working through these steps, you will be able to see the path forward more clearly and create a plan to help you move toward the things you want in your life.

To summarize the four principles from Part Two, these fundamental action steps that facilitate change are:

- Identify the thoughts and beliefs in the areas you are stuck in.
- Rewire your beliefs to what is *more* true.
- Create action steps to live out those new beliefs.
- Do this over time.

Next, I am going to simplify the four principles down into Ten Steps, and I will do that in two phases. Those two phases are called Break it Down and Rebuild It.

This is so exciting!! You are about to gain clarity and connect the dots so you can get to the root of why you are stuck. Then you can rebuild a new mindset that will help you reach your goals. My hope is that going through these steps will free you up to pursue the things that matter to you!

Another way of stating this process is: Break your old way down into its parts and then rebuild it.

Okay, it's your turn. This is your invitation to change.

It's just 10 small steps. It's work, but it's worth it.

Step 1.
 Identify your goals.

The benefit of this is knowing where you want to go and what you want it to look like. Knowing where you want to go clarifies and prioritizes your time, life, and choices for you.

Your Turn:
 What is it you want to accomplish? Where are you stuck? What do you want things to be like? Identify the area you want to grow in and what you want it to look like and write this down.

Step 2.
  You need feedback.

You actually get a lot of feedback in life; you just don't see it that way. During a tennis lesson, my friend and coach Greg once said, "The tennis ball is just feedback. You can look at where it went and get feedback about what you did. Not positive or negative, it's just feedback. It just tells you if you want to keep doing what you've been doing or try something else."

Now, take a look at your current results in the area you want to move forward. The benefit is seeing what you are currently doing is producing. Frankly, sometimes I kid myself thinking I am doing more than I am. Look at the results. You have everything you need right there in front of you.

Your Turn:
  In the area you want to grow, what is actually happening compared to what you want to see happen? Name all the things. Write for at least 30 minutes to give your brain a chance to explore this.

Step 3.
  Explore your way of operating and break it down.

Getting clarity on your way of doing things and operating is key to clearly seeing your old mindset. You can do this by **breaking it down into its parts**. Peeling apart and demystifying your way of operating into categories like thoughts, beliefs, and their fruit is going to allow you to see exactly the sequence of events that has you where you are.

Your Turn:

Turn back to the Flawed Mindset Worksheet and fill out your current way of operating, breaking it down into thoughts, beliefs, actions, and feelings. Fill out **each** category, and if you are unsure, look at the example to help you.

Step 4.
Connect the dots.

Once you have it down into its parts, discover your old way of doing things. You can begin to **connect the dots** by connecting your thoughts and beliefs to your behaviors and then to the results you have that you don't like. This will help you understand why you are where you are. There is no more confusion. It's right there. There is no more mystery. It's your mindset; it's your way of operating.

Your Turn:

How does your current situation connect with your Flawed Mindset? Make five connections between what is happening in your life with the series of beliefs, thoughts, feelings, and actions on your Flawed Mindset Worksheet. Write for 30 minutes to let your mind explore this.

Step 5.
Summarize your way of living life into a mindset.

This allows you to crystallize the way of operating that has produced the results you have so that you can recognize it in the moment.

Your Turn:

Come up with a fun and creative way to recognize your mindset. Naming it is one way to do this. Drawing it out in a person is another way.

Once you get to this point, it's very exciting but can feel a little uneasy. As I coach people through this process, I am always so excited because by this time they have two of the three big things behind them, they have discovered why they do what they do and have the awareness in the moment. What's left is the choices portion of the triad.

At this point, my clients have made so much progress and yet I can hear in their voices that they feel a little downcast. When I ask, I almost always hear, "Yes, I can see why I am stuck, but I don't see how to do things differently yet."

I get it. They don't see their way out. There isn't a path to change lit for them that feels great. If you can identify with this feeling, don't worry! That's where we are headed next in the rebuilding phase. Just like you clearly see the reason you are stuck now, you will also clearly see your way out from where you are. Trust me. I've done this hundreds of times.

20

Rebuild It

Steps 6-10

S tep 6.
Identify your positive anchor.

The best way for you to get a glimpse into your way out is to **identify the way you are doing something when you are doing it the way you want.** What do I mean by this? Do you remember my example of Lucy getting sick and my communication with Curt? That's my positive anchor. You have to find yours around the area where you are stuck. It's from a time when you can recall doing something the way you want to do it—or even having it modeled for you. This allows you to pinpoint and see your successful way of operating.

Your Turn:

Identify a time, moment, or season in your life when you did things the way you want to be doing them. A time when you were successful at the thing you want to change. Look back at Chapter

10 and explore this. Write down your thoughts and memories.

Step 7.
Identify your Mindset of Truth.

Now we are going to go through the same exercises we went through on the Flawed Mindset side. We are going to **break it down into its parts**. This allows you to see this way of operating in its categories and identify the way of thinking, believing, acting, and triggering yourself into this mindset.

Your Turn:

Turn back to the Mindset of Truth Worksheet and fill it out using your positive anchor experience. Break it down into thoughts, beliefs, actions, and feelings. Fill out **each** category, and if you are unsure, look at the example.

Step 8.
Connect the dots between your Mindset of Truth and your goals.

Rebuilding your new mindset allows you to begin to **connect your Mindset of Truth or new way of operating to a path forward toward your goals.** What do you need to be thinking, believing, and doing to reach "x" goal? Connect your thoughts and beliefs to your behaviors and then to the results you want.

Your Turn:

How does your goal connect with your Mindset of Truth?

Make five connections between your goal and your Mindset of Truth. See if you can draw a line from the thoughts and beliefs to your feelings and actions to the goals you stated in Step One or where you want to be in your life.

Step 9.

Write out your small action steps: daily, weekly, and monthly.

After we make these connections, **the next step is to create a plan that practices your Mindset of Truth and makes it actionable.** As we have discussed, these become automatic when you practice them over time. Make sure that in your thoughts, beliefs, and actions leading to the fruit you want in your life, there are small action steps for you to take that bridge the Mindset of Truth beliefs with the goals you want to accomplish. This isn't a repeat of the step before, it's just ensuring you have plenty of small actionable steps to take to achieve your goals.

Your Turn:

What are some small action steps that you could take over the course of six months to build a bridge from your Mindset of Truth to your goals?

Now that you have spent time rebuilding a new mindset, let's pause and look back over your goals and make sure they are still where you want to go. **By reaffirming and tweaking** your goals, you gain clarity on what you want your goals to be and what it will look like when you get there. This helps you connect your new mindset to where you are headed and ensure they are all aligned.

Step 10.

Work on your small action steps and keep going even if you miss a day or a week.

Finally, with the over-time principle, you will be aiming in the right direction, moving one step at a time toward your goal. Give it time to see the results. Don't make a plan and stick to it for a week or a month and abandon it because you aren't seeing the results you want. Make a plan and plan to stick with it. Intentionally not looking for the results to show up for three to six months will allow you to be free to build a new way of doing things and give your new actions time to bear fruit.

Your Turn:

Not to be trite, but don't quit. Stay on the track. Keep to your plan.

Now you have completed reading the Ten Steps. I know how I would approach reading them. If you are like me, you wanted to get through to the end to see what the secret sauce was to decide if you want to invest the time in them. No, I am not reading your journal or your mind. I would be doing the same thing. So, I am going to take the liberty of making a recommendation.

Because change takes work plus time, my recommendation is this.

1. Set aside each week to do one step.
2. Schedule two or three 30-minute sessions and spend that time thinking about the step and exploring the questions, writing down your answers.

I know some will take more time or work than others, but 30 minutes can be a rule of thumb. Giving yourself time and space to work is so beneficial. At that pace, you will be finished with the Ten Steps in two-and-a-half months, and that's a great pace for making some significant mindset shifts. I am going to ask you to trust me that doing the work will change your mindset and help you move toward your goals.

I want to end with something significant and very personal from my own life—an area where I had a Flawed Mindset that was part of what kept me stuck for years. Changing my mindset did actually change my circumstances, but how much was my mindset and the changes I made, and how much was God, I'll let you decide.

21

Explore Reality

About 10 years ago, my best friend, Jen, and I went to a four-day conference called Explore Reality. In hindsight, it was a group coaching weekend, and by group, I mean around 40 people. In preparation for the weekend, we had calls with different people to gain clarity on what we wanted to get out of the long weekend. They said the people with clear goals got the most out of it. Being a good student, going in, I was pretty clear on my three things. Number one, I was in my mid-40s, and I had done a fair amount of work on all the reasons why I might be single—I wanted to know if there was anything else that I needed to see that was standing in my way. As I reflect back, I was like a baby duck sitting in front of a band of angry hippos. I was about to be on the belly side of a stampede. Reasons number two and three went by the wayside.

Oh, it's funny now.

On day two, 40 grown adults were all sitting in a large circle facing one another. It was like an extra-large AA meeting. This is a good lesson too—in order to get help you have to raise your hand and say you want it. So, I did. The first principle they taught was that you get out of things what you put into them. I was in, sort of. I raised my hand and stood up. They said, "Hi, how can we support you?" I went on to say something like, "I'm Cynthia and I am in my mid-40s and want to be married and I have done a fair amount of work and just want to know if there is anything I am missing that is in the way." I mean that's such an innocent statement in my opinion. And then came the hammer.

Ennio said, "Well tell us more about that." And then I exposed my mindset around dating. "I hate dating. I'd rather be on a walk, listening to a good audiobook, or walking with my dogs on a pretty day than going on a date with somebody I don't know." I might as well have lofted him a tennis ball and said, "Please, hit this ball to the moon."

And he did.

Suffice it to say that their feedback was excellent. How can you get to know someone when you are chronically and critically evaluating them for the next date? What about sitting across from another human being made in the image of God and getting to know them? Asking the other 38 members of my cohort, Ennio said, "How many of you know when you are being judged?" The hands went up. "How does that make you react?" The group blurted out, "Closed up, not able to share, nervous, not able to be yourself." Well, my mindset around dating was so completely narrow that evidently, I was an unsafe person to be yourself with because I was on the other side constantly trying to figure out if I wanted to go out again. And I am sure they were on the other side, thinking, "This is an easy no." As it turns out, my mindset around dating was similar to the game "Would You Rather." If you are a parent and haven't played this with your kids, you should. Would you rather lose your sight or your hearing? Would you rather drown or be killed by bees? Would you rather go on a blind date or poke your eyes out? You get my drift.

Anyway, that was my mindset. It was a game of "Would You Rather," and it took a really special someone to win that game for me. I had spent years nursing and adding to my game unknowingly.

After Explore Reality, I realized I was the problem. I entered every date thinking about whether I could marry this guy or if I even wanted to spend another two to five hours with him. I wasn't just getting to know him, enjoying the moment and the experience. There was none of that because I had built a pretty big wall that kept my little castle safe and fun and only involving what I wanted to do.

It's hilarious now. I am sure those of you who are married with kids are wondering when the last time anything was about you and what you wanted to do. My mindset was killing my dating life, which ultimately kept me single until I was 53.

After seeing this, it was SO hopeful because I realized I had some changing to do. First, I had to reconstruct my mindset about dating. Forget marriage, because at the rate and trajectory I was going, I wasn't going to get there.

So, I did. First, I changed my beliefs and my thoughts, and that changed my feelings and my actions. I started by setting down a rule for myself that I had to date someone for three months and spend the time with them getting to know them. I challenged myself to take my evaluation hat off and instead see them as human beings made in the image of God and worthy of being known.

For the record, I believe the Lord had everything to do with me finding my husband because it was eight years after I went to that conference and made a ton of changes that I met Curt. In other words, it didn't cure all right away. In fact, I wanted to throw in the towel several times. Simultaneously, I believe God used my willingness to go to a place I had poo-pooed for years because I had been too snooty or unable to handle my own awkwardness to attend the gathering of singles at church. And at just the right time, in September of 2021, at the ripe age of 53, the Lord orchestrated our meeting.

22

The Next Step

his book is intended to be a first step. The next step if you want one is my coaching curriculum, called The Link Program, which is for those who want to go deeper. I have taken so many people through the program and when we aren't going through it page by page, I am walking them through it, unbeknownst to them. If this book didn't quite get you where you want to go, The Link Program is a more in-depth course that will take you step by step through this process, including worksheets, exercises, and videos to come in 2024. You can find it at https://linklifecoaching.com or https://cynthiabaker.com.

The four principles of change are included as well as a few of the exercises I've shared here. It will hold your hand, so to speak, toward meeting your goals as you go through 17 different lessons, starting with identifying what your goals are, the patterns you developed from childhood, and understanding the skills you learned to get you where you are. It will help you understand how you approach hard things, relationships, and life and gain clarity on how you learned to navigate the world.

It will lead you to connect the dots between your patterns and how you are stuck and understand the barriers to reaching your goals. Along the way, you will identify what needs to change to meet your goals, and just as you identified the mindset that has you stuck, it will lead you to identify the Mindset of Truth and a plan to be where you want to be in life.

It is my sincere hope that this book has accomplished three things.

Number one, if you are stuck, the mystery as to why has been removed. Number two, you believe there is a path to change. And lastly, number three, you believe that the work is worth it.

I am so grateful and to clients who allowed me to share their stories and to the hundreds of others that I have had the privilege of working with toward the things they want in their lives.

This is the one and only life God gave you, and you have a ton to offer this crazy world. I pray you will get the healing you need. I pray you will do the work that is only yours to do. Lastly, I pray that you will enjoy living out of your Mindset of Truth in a way that blesses you and the world around you.

On God & Change

As I look at my own experiences and reflect on others I've coached, one of the problems I see is that people think it is incongruent to need to "do" something in their own healing process. Isn't it all on God? In my faith as a follower of Jesus, the Scriptures say that Jesus plus nothing we do equals our restoration to God. We do not do anything to earn our salvation. It is by faith alone, as is our sanctification (a.k.a. transformation). In light of that, it seems confusing to say that we actually have to do something to change.

As I have wrestled with what the Scriptures say, I believe we are talking about separate issues. What I think this book is talking about is the way God works in the world. I don't even begin to understand this concept in its totality, by the way, but what I do know is that as I read and observe God's Word, there are several laws at work together that do not contradict one another.

One is the law of sowing and reaping. In our world, God has ordained that we reap a harvest of our choices, both good and bad. (This is not a promise because that would negate trust in God. We all know there are exceptions—consider farmers who lose their crops after hard seasons of planting and watering, the healthy man or woman who gets sick with cancer, and the list goes on.) To say we control the outcome is also taking a principle and going too far with it.

Another way we see God at work in His Word is through the story of His relationship with us. The word "relationship" is key because it implies that there are two participants. Throughout the Scriptures, we see stories of God and man together working toward an outcome. For example, Adam and Eve named the animals and toiled over the ground God created; the angels told Joseph to take Mary and Jesus and flee to Egypt; and Aaron and Hur held up Moses' arms to ensure victory for the Israelites. Again, the list goes on. In this principle, like with sowing and reaping, ultimately God's plan is accomplished, so to say it is wholly dependent on us cooperating with God is also taking a principle too far.

Getting unstuck feels more like a few of the commands and principles God has given us; seeing the connection to neuroscience's study of the brain 100% affirms these principles and that they can yield the fruit we want in our lives. For example, how to get unstuck and live happily and blessed with peace and joy, knowing there are circumstances, people, and things including our own bodies, that we cannot control. It's a mystery to be sure; we cannot control things and yet we have some agency in the outcome of the adventure of our lives alongside the Creator of the universe and others He brings along our paths.

Remember, this process hasn't prepared you never to struggle again, so don't be discouraged when you fail. Failure is a part of life, and so is moving forward. This process will hopefully help you identify the old ways that have you stuck so that you can shift over to your Mindset of Truth and make different choices that ultimately will produce the fruit in keeping with your goals. Your goals will be reached one choice at a time, one day at a time, and you have to do the hard work to identify both where you want to go and what has been in the way.

Know that we all struggle and fall back at any given moment. Achieving your goals is about not reacting to those failures but recognizing and choosing the things to trigger you into your Mindset of Truth, ultimately linking you to what can be.

I have seen firsthand that all four of the principles in this process are crucial to change. As I said, I think the reason people stay stuck in areas of their lives is because they never do all four of the principles at the same time, over time. One of the coolest things that happened to me as I worked on this book was seeing that the research in the world of neuroscience 100% supported the principles and commands the Lord gave to us in the Scriptures. Actually, it floored me and grew my faith in Jesus.

I realized He doesn't always give us a "why" behind His commands but has allowed us to discover that the commands and principles He has given us are at a minimum connected to how He made our brains. I hope that a byproduct of this book has been an increased faith in your Creator. That would have been worth every moment.

Yours Truly,

Cynthia

Notes

WHY ALL THE MYSTERY?

1   Stiller, Ben. 2013. The Secret Life of Walter Mitty. United States: Twentieth Century Fox.

MY BRAIN IS MORE GENIUS THAN I AM

2   Lyon, Jason. 2019 September 24. To Pay Attention, the Brain Uses Filters, Not a Spotlight. Quantummagazine.org, https://www.quantamagazine.or g/to-pay-attention-the-brain-uses-filters-not-a-spotlight-20190924/

3   Neurotrack. "Your Brain's Autopilot Function." Accessed October 28, 2023. https://neurotrack.com/resources/your-brains-autopilot-function#:~:t ext=The%20basal%20ganglia%2C%20a%20group,even%20if%20you% 20feel%20motivated.

4   StartUp Health. "The Neuroscience of Behavior Change." Accessed October 28, 2023. https://healthtransformer.co/the-neuroscience-of-behavior-c hange-bcb567fa83c1#:~:text=Neural%20pathways%2C%20comprised% 20of%20neurons,or%20roads%20in%20our%20brain.

5   Dr. Jane Gardner, Mindset for Success (Allen, Texas. The Gardner Institute).

6   StartUp Health. "The Neuroscience of Behavior Change." Accessed October 28, 2023. https://healthtransformer.co/the-neuroscience-of-behavior-c hange-bcb567fa83c1#:~:text=Neural%20pathways%2C%20comprised% 20of%20neurons,or%20roads%20in%20our%20brain.

7   Gretchen Rubin, Better Than Before, What I Learned About Making And Breaking Habits – To Sleep More, Quit Sugar, Procrastinate Less, and Generally Build A Happier Life. (New York, New York. Broadway Books, 2015) 117.

8   Columbia. Columbia University Irving Medical Center. "Baby Neurons in Adult Brains are Needed to Maintain Memory." Accessed October 23, 20203. https://www.cuimc.columbia.edu/news/baby-neurons-adult-bra ins-are-needed-maintain-memory#:~:text=Researchers%20estimate%

20that%20the%20brain%27s,neurons%20each%20day%20throughout
%20adulthood.

9   Dr. Caroline Leaf, Switch on Your Brain, The Key to Peak Happiness,
    Thinking and Health (Grand Rapids, MI: Baker Books, 2013, 63.

HOW MINDSETS FORM

10 The Attachment Project. "What is Attachment Theory?" Accessed October
    23, 2023. https://www.attachmentproject.com/attachment-theory/

11 Good Therapy. "Understanding the Brain's Tendency to Manufacture
    Information." Accessed October 23, 2023. https://www.goodtherapy.org/
    blog/taming-the-brain-0228125/

YOU HAVE AGENCY!

12 Open Education Sociology Dictionary. (n.d.). Agency. Open Education
    Sociology Dictionary. Retrieved October 20, 2023, from https://sociolo
    gydictionary.org/agency/#definition_of_agency.

13 Elizabeth Gilbreath, Big Magic, Creative Living Beyond Fear (New York, NY:
    Riverhead Books, 2015) 26.

WE ALWAYS HAVE CHOICES

14 Luke 6:27-31 (NIV)

15 Hall, B., Stoltz, E. (2014, September 21). Pilot 1 (Season 1, Episode 1).
    [Madam Secretary Episode 1]. Morgan Freeman. Madam Secretary. Barbara
    Hall Productions Revelations Entertainment CBS Television Studios.

PRINCIPLE ONE

16 Antanaityte, Neringa. "Mind Matters: How To Effortlessly Have More
    Positive Thoughts." TLEXInstitute.com. TLEX Institute. (accessed April
    3, 2023). https://tlexmindmatters.com/how-to-effortlessly-have-more-
    positive-thoughts/

17 Patrias K. Citing medicine: the NLM style guide for authors, editors, and
    publishers [Internet]. 2nd ed. Wendling DL, technical editor. Bethesda
    (MD): National Library of Medicine (US); 2007 - [updated 2016 Sept 8;
    cited 2023, Oct 12]. Available from: https://www.ncbi.nlm.nih.gov/books/
    NBK279297/.

18 2 Cor 10:3-6 (NIV)

19 Chandler, Matt. "Exodus (Part 11)—Just Men." Sermon,The Village Church,
    Flower Mound, Texas, November 6, 2016.

20 Ibid.

21 Ibid.

22 Darren Hardy, The Compound Effect, Jumpstart Your Income, Your Life, Your Success (New York, NY: Vanguard Press, 2010) 10.

23 Ibid.

24 Leaf, Switch on Your Brain, 35.

25 Dr. Jane Gardner, Mindset for Success (Allen, Texas. The Gardner Institute).

26 Leaf, Switch on Your Brain, 175.

YOUR OWN PERSONAL ANCHOR

27 Henry Kimsey-House et al., Co-Active Coaching: Changing Business, Transforming Lives Third Edition (Boston and London: Nicholas Brealey Publishing, 2011), xvi.

28 Ibid.

PRINCIPLE TWO

29 Rom 12:2 (NIV)

30 Merriam-Webster.com Dictionary, s.v. "renew," accessed April 1, 2023, merriam-webster.com/dictionary/renew.

31 Leaf, Switch on Your Brain, 151.

32 Phil 4:8 (AMP)

33 American Psychological Association. (n.d.). Neuroplasticity. In APA dictionary of psychology. Retrieved October 18, 2023, from https://dict ionary.apa.org/neural-plasticity.

34 Psychology Today (n.d.) Neuroplasticity. In Psychology Today. Retrieved October 18, 2023, from https://www.psychologytoday.com/us/basics/neur oplasticity.

35 Leaf, Switch on Your Brain, 63.

36 "Vocabulary.com Dictionary" s.v. "focus," accessed April 1, 2023, https://w ww.vocabulary.com/dictionary/focus.

PRINCIPLE THREE

37 John 13:14-17 (AMP)

38 John 13:17 (AMPC)

39 Phil 4:9 (AMPC)

40 Phil 4:9 (AMP)

41 Leaf, Switch on Your Brain, 197.

42 Ibid.

43 Ibid.

44 Wikipedia contributors, "Cognitive behavioral therapy," Wikipedia, The Free Encyclopedia, en.wikipedia.org/wiki/Cognitive_behavioral_therapy (accessed April 2, 2023).

45 Keller, Timothy. "295. "Resting Grace." Timothy Keller Sermons Podcast by Gospel in Life. Podcast audio, September 9, 2019. https://podcast.gospe linlife.com/e/resting-grace/.

46 Exodus 17:9-14 (NIV)

PRINCIPLE FOUR

47 Angela Duckworth, Grit, The Power of Passion and Perseverance. (New York, New York, Simon & Schuster, Inc., 2016), 39.

48 Carey Lohrenz, Fearless Leadership (Second Edition): High-Performance Lessons from the Flight Deck. (United States: Greenleaf Book Group Press, 2014), 64.

49 Lohrenz, Fearless Leadership, 39.

50 Hani, Julie. "The Neuroscience of Behavior Change." https://healthtransfo rmer.co/the-neuroscience-of-behavior-change-bcb567fa83c1 (accessed April 7,2023).

51 Ibid.

52 Gal 6:7-9 (NIV)

53 Phil 4:9 (AMP)

54 John 13:17 (AMP)

FOUR PRINCIPLES AND TEN STEPS

55 Leaf, Switch on Your Brain, 197.

About the Author

Cynthia Baker is passionate about helping people uncover what's holding them back and experience the excitement of unlocking their potential and reaching their goals. Drawing from years of professional coaching and counseling experience, Cynthia specifically designed the Link program to help clients connect the dots between the way they think and how they act. When people see how their mindsets fit together with their behaviors and the results they experience, they can finally make lasting changes in the places they've been stuck.

Raised in Tyler, Texas, Cynthia graduated from the University of Texas at Austin in 1992. In 2002, after seven years in the financial world, Cynthia left corporate America to attend Dallas Theological Seminary, where she received her Master's in Biblical Counseling. She has spent the last two decades working with and developing people in a variety of settings, from counseling and recovery practice, church ministry, and now coaching individuals, small businesses, corporate teams and CEOs.

Cynthia loves helping people get "unstuck" so they can pursue a life that brings joy. As a follower of Jesus, she loves inviting people to experience the freedom that God has for their lives. Her free time usually involves family, friends and outdoor activities (and typically coffee). She loves hanging out with her people – including her husband, Curt, a very rambunctious teenage boy, Lincoln and her dogs, Clara and Lucy.

You can connect with me on:

🌐 https://cynthiabaker.com

Subscribe to my newsletter:

✉ https://linklifecoaching.com

Also by Cynthia Baker

The Link Program
https://cynthiabaker.com/the-link-program

Drawing from years of professional coaching and counseling experience, Cynthia specifically designed the Link program to help clients connect the dots between the way they think and how they act. When people see how their mindsets fit together with their behaviors and the results they experience, they can finally make lasting changes in the places they've been stuck.